Poetry To Warm The Heart With

by

Werner W.J.F. Toelen

authorHOUSE™

1663 LIBERTY DRIVE, SUITE 200
BLOOMINGTON, INDIANA 47403
(800) 839-8640
WWW.AUTHORHOUSE.COM

First published by AuthorHouse 07/30/04

ISBN: 1-4184-8013-4 (sc)

Printed in the United States of America
Bloomington, Indiana

This book is printed on acid-free paper.

Vow To My Girl

Baby how we met.
I just can't forget.
I still feel you so close.
You're the one I love the most.
I know this love will never go away.
Because every night and day I pray.
I have seen you in my dream.
Your head is on my shoulder when you lean.
We know what's between you and me.
There's nobody that can break us apart you'll see.
This love is stronger than before.
When you're down I'll pick you up off the floor.
I want to hold you in my arms very tight.
While the sun slowly fade into the night.
I promise I'll do it all slow.
Cause I don't want to let this feeling go.
Marry me and you'll see.
You're the one that makes me happy and free.
Can't stop thinking of you every day.
And that is the last thing that I want to say.

Missing

You're the air that I breathe.
Cause you're the one that I need.
The sun is on my face.
In every alley and every place.
There is a bright face in the moon right up in the sky.
That face reminds me of my girl that I miss, and I started to cry.
You're my warmth in the winters when it's freezing cold.
You're my artic breeze in the hot summer and that's worth more to me then gold.
Please understand and know that I'll never leave you.
Our love is ment to be; and my feelings are true.

Marry Me Baby

We belong together.
From today and forever.
This is the right thing to do.
Baby I truly love you.
When I have to leave and be on my way.
I'll keep you in my heart throughout the day.
I see your face in the moonlight every night.
I'm going to hold you close to me very tight.
Today I kneeled down for you. .
And I know you'll say; "YES I DO".
Please take this ring and marry me.
We're not for two but for three.
So lets get married even today.
And stay together till we're old and gray.

Never Give You Up

My heart I give it to you entirely.
Even my mind, body and soul you're getting it freely.
I'll hold you so very tight.
And I'll kiss you with passion in the moonlight.
Cause I never want to lose you out of my life.
And if I did, it would hurt me! Like I've been cut with a knife.
I know our love is close and strong.
Without you everything would go wrong.
Never going to give our love a break.
My love for you is no mistake.
Even though things are going bad.
Or when one of us gets mad or sad.
We'll win from all the pain.
You know I am the sun after the rain.

A Far Away X-Mass Love

This x-mass is with a tear.
Cause you're not here.
I miss my love.
Now I'm praying to the angles above.
This x-mass we're far apart.
Yet you're always in my heart.
So a letter to Santa I'll send for you.
You'll get a gift that's the best that I can do.
So baby this x-mass will start with a new beginning you'll see.
With a song of love that lay's deep within me.
Tears of joy the first time we meet.
Cause Santa takes you in his seat.
The next morning you opened my front door.
And you where walking across my floor.
To the room where you know I sleep.
Your heart is pounding hard and deep.
You climbed in bed next to me that night.
So I'd wake up next to you in the early morning light.
And when I open my eyes and you're the one I seen.
I said baby you have the heart of a queen.

You're The One

You're the one I'll love forever.
Cause our souls bond us together.
Never had a feeling like this.
Now I'm longing for your touch and your kiss.
I'll wait till the time is right to be there.
It's my love I want to share.
Luck is by my side.
And love will be our guide.
I'll never let you go I'm here to stay.
That's why every night I go to God and pray.
I ask him never let this love fade away.
I can't live no more without you not even for a single day.
A life without you I can't bare.
You know my heart is already there.
You have all my love.
And you said to me master you're my angel from above.
I won't and I can't let this feeling go.
Because baby our son and I love you so.
When I look in your eyes I see the future that may come along.
Baby please listens to the music our love is in every song.

Key To My Heart

I have lonely hours and lonely days.
That's what I feel when I must leave or getaway.
Everyday and night I'm thinking about you constantly.
Cause your heart is beating inside of me.
I see that we're meant to be.
Our love is for eternity.
I gave you the key to my heart.
And when you're gone my world will be torn apart.
So please never ever leave me or go away.
You're the one that I love forever and a day.
You have my key to my heart and soul.
Unlock it and let my feeling come under control.

Goddess You'll Stay In Our Hearts

Goddess you're the one I want to hear all day long.
Till you get sleepy or you're gone.
I know we're getting better every day.
And sometime a poem is how I speak out my lost words to say.
You're so sweet and I want you to be my friend forever.
You said I'm kind of a romantic poetic and a little clever.
My heart is filled with joy when I hear you talking in the chat
room.
You're always sweet even when you stand into the light of the
moon.
I never seen your face but I don't care.
I love you like a friend here or even there.

I Love You With All I Have

Your eyes are colored like the trees in the fall.
Your love stands like a tree very tall.
I love you and I'll walk through hell.
Yes baby I think you're very swell.
The smile on your face warms me up when I'm cold.
This is a strong feeling that I want to hold.
Your love is so pure and fine.
We belong together like a good old bottle of red wine.
So here we are distant lovers but oh so close.
Baby you the one I love the most.
We'll be together no matter what road we may take.
And God may strike me with lightning if I make a mistake.

Heartbeat

I'll lay you down in our bed.
Like the first day we wed.
We're so close together.
Your son and I are bonded forever.
You're my world and my light.
I'll always be in your sight.
You make my heart beat so fast.
I know that our love will forever last.
We take things nice and slow so we know our love will slowly
grow.
That's the reason why we let our love show.
I want to surprise you with a poem every day.
I love you is all I want to say.
So take this journey deep inside.
Come on baby lets go for a ride.
Now we're away from it all it's just you and I.
On a bench in the forest you lean to me and start to cry.
I love the way you are and the way you make me feel.
You make my heart alive because you broke the wall of steel.
I'll love you forever.
God baby you're so clever.
We'll stay together till we're old and gray.
I'll love you forever and a day.

Friends In Need

A Friend who is in desperate need.
You feel sad when there heart starts to bleed.
You try your best to make them feel okay.
When they lost a love their friends are here to stay.
True friendship never falls apart.
Cause true friendship comes from the heart.
The best way to find out is my friend for real.
Is to use your mind and heart to feel.
So when you need your special friend.
They stick to you till the end.
They help the best with what they can do.
Cause you're their best friend to.
So when your down and you cant get back on your feet.
They're here to help you as fast as a heartbeat.
Your best friends never let you down at all.
You know even at midnight you may call.
And when I need help and I can't beat my problems alone.
I call on my friend's cause they're like a brother or sister of my own.

Dreaming

When I look into your eyes.
My mind starts to fantasize.
I'm thinking of the day that we're going to meet.
Oh Lord that would be neat.
Can't wait to wrap my arms around you.
Yes honeybee that's the first thing I want to do.
We'll meet each other somewhere.
Baby when and how I don't care.
I know we're joining our souls into one heart.
I need you in my life so don't keep this love apart.

Sing

When I sing I do it for you.
Like lovers are suppose to do.
Every word I say I mean it from deep inside.
Girl your eyes are like stars and the moonlight, don't be shy and
hide.
I sing of love that I never felt before.
Now I won't stop I need you even more.
I won't stop loving you.
Cause my heart said you just can't do.
There will be one day in my life.
I'll ask you to marry me and be my wife.
I'll never give up not even stop.
My love will never drop.
No interfering will be there.
I promise you yes I swear.
The love between us is the best thing I see.
I LOVE YOU with all my heart, mind, and soul like you do me.

Net

I met you in the bi-1 room on yahoo.
The 1-day I ask to sweetcandygirl62 how are you.
We talked for long hours and long days.
I felt ok with room 1 of the both ways.
In the beginning things where wrong.
But your love was already strong.
You let me choose between two people I love.
The choice was you cause I love you like an angel from above.
And a friend helped us in every way.
He even does it still today.
3 way talk about all things in life.
He cyber married us now you're my wife.
A double wedding it was so neat.
Now I can't wait till we meet.
Days will fly and our loves will grow.
We live every day with our love and we let the time flow.

Best Friends

I'm just a message away.
Here I am and I'm going to stay.
I really don't go anywhere.
Cause my friends; I am here and I care.
When you're hurt, sick or even sad.
I won't go to bed until you're glad.
You can call me on the phone.
My friends you know you're never alone.
I'll even fly to you when you need me there.
This I promise to you yes I swear.
The love I have for my best's friends.
They'll stay in my heart and it never ends.

Love's Better Then Lust

When you really love some one.
It's happiness and fun.
You'll walk through fire for their lives.
And they'll be surprised.
Love is better then lust.
Cause love isn't a must.
Love is between two people with a pure heart and soul.
Like my lover she makes my world whole.
I love her every day.
And I won't walk away.
We've taken a vow together.
Yes I love my girl from November 14th even better.

Far Away

You're there and I'm here.
We're bond by love anger and fear.
Everyday we've come closer together.
Even in the sun or the rainy weather.
The days are passing slowly away.
Damn I wish you could stay.
You know I'll wait till the end of time.
And when you're here then we'll drink a glass of wine.
No matter how you look.
I know you're life is like an open book.
Open the page and I can read between every line.
Yes we'll come together in the end of time.
I'll fly to you.
Cause for you there's nothing I wouldn't do.
I want to be forever in your sight.
In the sunshine or even the moonlight.
Wherever you may go.
You must know.
My love is for you every day.
You'll receive more love when I come your way.

Remember Me

Why is the reason I died?
I never ever lied.
My trust is here.
Please don't feel my fear.
You're always going to be my friend.
I know you understand.
I'm real close by.
Even after I die.
Never forget the things I said.
Cause memories are always in your head.
When I was here.
My friends were always so close and near.
I was the shoulder when you needed to cry.
It didn't matter when you never told me the reason why.
I know the best days never will be astray.
I love you all forever and a day.

Friends

You're our friend.
Now and always and even till the end.
We love you my friend with all our heart.
You're a friend right from the start.
You're our brother and we'll never drift away.
You leaned on us right from the first day.
We're here for you I just want you to know.
Just a little message is enough to say hello.
We're here for you please know that well.
Lets talk about life and all will be swell.
Don't hesitate because you know you're our friend.
Because our friendship is gold we'll stick till the end.

Pain

You hold your pain so much inside.
Let them out let them slide.
Cause if you hold your fears so tight.
You'll never see the bright light.
So release your fears and feelings out to space.
Then you'll feel the sunshine on your face.
Once you let your fears go and you opened your heart you'll see.
That your life will feel much happier and free.

Love Your Poems

My baby gave words to me.
And now you'll see.
Her words are good.
Just like soul food.
Never let it fade away.
It's your love that makes me stay.
I love you with every word you say.
Same like I, you love me in any kind of way.
See you move me even more.
That's why I love you even better then before.
And the words you say is like gold to me.
With you I want to grow old beyond eternity.

In Memory Of Badgirl

She came and joins the room.
Her death was just to soon.
This girl was just 20 years old.
And she had no fears but a heart of gold.
We can't believe that she's gone.
Dying at a young age like this was wrong.
Why is it that we meet people that are nice?
Her death brought us in a down mood not once but twice.
Her music was very smooth and great.
When we met her it was just by fate.
Her presents felt like a vibe of love.
She is now with God and his angels above.
The memories of you will stay in our heart.
We keep you there so we're never far apart.
You're a star up in heaven above.
And people will remember that special love.
We all didn't know you very well.
Yet you was very nice we all could tell.
We took you in our hearts my friend.
We'll cherish you till our lives entirely end.

Love Your Son

I met a girl on the Internet oh my God we had lots of fun.
Then suddenly she told me baby I have a son.
She was thinking now my Internet lover is going to walk away.
And all the love is gone in just one day.
I said what's his name & age, can I see a picture of his face.
Damn he's so cute I wish I could be there at your place.
That girl and her son took my heart that day.
Sometimes I close my eyes and I see us play.
Fighting with swords or picking him up and making him fly.
Baby I love your son his words makes me cry.
Why is it that this girl and her son love me so much?
Is it the place in there hearts that I had touched?
I never will hurt those two.
I simply just can't do.
That little boy makes funny faces and he makes me smile and cry.
I know I can never leave them cause I would rather die.
That girl and her son are a gift from heaven above.
Come here you two and give me a hug, cause this is real love.

New Daddy

To My Little Sport

I met this girl she has a cute little guy.
That little guy listens to me, sometimes I wondering why.
Since he let me in as a new daddy in his little heart.
We bonded together and I'll never tear this apart.
The connection between us is unique and rare.
And with Halloween I'll try to be there.
Then him and I can trick and treat on Halloween night.
We'll walk side by side in the moonlight.
I know he will love this special day.
We'll have fun in every kind of way.
And maybe his mother will come to.
Cause I, as his new daddy loves her that's so true.
Can't wait till that day will come.
Yes little sport I love you like my own son.

Valentines Day

I want to share my finest thoughts together with you.
I love you so much you know this is true.
That's why on Valentine's Day.
I have some sweet words I like to say.
I still can remember where we first met the very first time.
Maybe it sound possessive but you're all mine.
You asked me to marry you and I was shocked.
I gave you the key to my heart cause it was locked.
I hope to see you in life for real.
I'll be your knight in amour of gold but not of steel.
I promise you I'll never let you go.
Yes baby I love you so.
I know you'll love my gift and a card with a Valentines rhyme.
Perhaps it's not much but for you I would spend my last dime.
So I wish you a very nice Valentines Day.
My Valentine I love you and that is all I wanted to say.

Without You I'll Die

Girl what must I do.
I just can't live without you.
Without your love I'm going to die.
The only thing I do is cry.
I love you and sometimes I don't know the words to say.
My heart tells me I love you forever and a day.
I see the stars and the moon in the sky I declare.
They're like you pretty far, and it's not fair!
Soon I'll come to you.
Cause my love for you is so true.

My Lovers' Words To Me

On November 14th I want this to rhyme.
My baby gave me more then her time.
She gave me a life for me to see.
I want her to be my wife so people let me free.
When I look in her eyes all I want to say.
Baby hold me I want you every day.
You are my life, my air that I breathe.
I know your love is strong that's why I can never leave.
You gave me your heart and set me free.
You're the one that's saved me from all the horrible things that
happened to me.
You're my life cause your name is always in my mind.
Baby I want to be there and stay, never leave me here behind!
You're in my heart I feel you so deep within.
I want to hold you skin to skin.
You're my lover for the rest of my life.
Marry me baby; I want you to be my wife.

Some Words To My Lover

These are some words I want to reveal.
About a girl that I love so much that's for real.
I want to tell her what I feel inside.
Can't live without my girl and God will be our guide.
Sometimes its hard cause my words are so slim.
When we're not together my love is like a light that shines so dime.
I open my heart for my baby every day.
Cause I love her in every kind of way.
She took me in her heart and now I'm not sad.
She brings joy to my life and now I'm glad.
I gave her more than most girls could get.
I gave her my heart from the moment we met.
I've taken this girl's son into my heart like he's my own.
That's why I can't wait till I'm back home.
I put this girl on a high throne.
I know she will never leave me alone.
Darling I gave this poem to you.
That's the least that I can do.
You're my queen and I'll be your king.
I kneel down before you please except this ring.

Six Sense

When I'm at work my girl set's by the phone.
I know she hates to be alone.
I miss her just as much.
In my mind I feel her touch.
I know she thinks of me so bad.
All her feelings are coming in my head.
I know when she is kissing my lips.
Or when she touches my skin with her fingertips.
With my mind I touch her and she can feel shivers over her skin.
It feels like heaven, we don't believe it's a sin.
Her hands are sliding on my chest and through my hair.
Baby it feels like I'm really there.
Our mind has a telepathic connection that's what we feel.
Some people think its weird but we know its real.
I feel you miles away I know that's okay.
I can only pray to see you some day.
Until that day we'll meet.
Our love in our minds is neat and sweet.

You're My Angel

I'm crazy in love.
She's my angel from above.
I never met a person so good for me.
She took my heart and set me free.
I'm sitting behind my computer I don't have to hide.
I'm so lucky that this girl takes me the way I'm inside.
At first I hid my face to afraid to let her see.
Oh my God I can't let her go I want her so bad with me.
Yes I made a mistake and I was wrong.
I just can't understand why her love is so strong.
Most girls would run away.
Seems my love for her made her stay.
I blush when she say's I'm cute and smart.
Girl you're the best thing in my life, that's why I love you with all
my heart.

Winters Touch

Baby let me touch your face.
I want to caress your body in every place.
We lay down side by side.
This feeling I have within I can't hide.
I'll Stroke your body till you want me more.
You start to moan harder then before.
I need your body completely; yes I want it all.
I lifted you up and place you against the wall.
I moved one of your legs up in the air.
I want to infiltrate you, then I stop when you're almost there.
Now I'll lay you down on a rug of bearskin.
And I let myself slide deep within.
Making love in front of an open fire.
You're the one, my only hearts desire.
Baby I can't hold on any more.
Lets come together on the bearskin rug on the floor.
Our climax ends with a touch.
Last words I said to you: I love you so much.
I'll hold you tight as we fall a sleep.
You're the one that I want for life to keep.

Passion Kiss

I feel fire in your kiss.
It's like a lightning bliss.
While I let my hands tease your body and soul.
I Love it when you come down and take control.
Your body moves like the sea.
Baby you so great when you make love with me.
Your Body starts to sweat.
We make love and not only in bed.
On a table or a chair.
Love your hands that slide through my hair.
Your nails are running on my back.
And I'll kiss you on your neck.
Feel the motion.
It's like the ocean.
From slow till fast.
This love will ever last.
The climax comes to our top.
I hear you say; baby don't stop.
Then we lie down and kiss together.
Baby I love you, always and forever.

Very Soon

I have a girlfriend she's so into my heart.
God I hate it that we live so far apart.
My love for her is so strong in every kind of way.
I know we could never part not even for a day.
She makes me smile and I know there's no denial.
She loves me so much and that's why we both smile.
We try to hold each other for a while.
It seems that every day we go through a trial.
Yet we know we'll meet each other very soon.
Then we'll walk by the light of the moon.

I'll Be Here Waiting For You

I'll be here waiting for you.
I know it's a hard thing to do.
I know you're so far away.
Yes I can fly in just one day.
I know you're there, and I'm still here.
It's all about trust and having no fear.
Whatever you do.
I'm here waiting for you.
We're oceans apart.
Yet you stay always in my heart.
I dream every night about you.
Girl I miss you and some times I don't know what to do.
Every word in a letter I write its straight from my heart.
You're in my life forever and I won't let us be torn apart.
Now I'm waiting here for you.
It's the best thing to do.
From the bottom of my heart I love you forever.
I just can't wait till we're together.

As Time Goes By

I'll wait for you.
For you my heart is true.
My heart will never be a prize you can win.
Someone already has my heart so I could never let another lover in.
Cause what we have is all good and true.
You're the one that loves me and yes I love you to.
You're my only love.
You're my angel that was sent to me from above.
You let me feel and make me see.
That this is the kind of love that was ment to be.
You're the best that I could ever get.
Our love is so good there's no regret.
This love is very special right from the start.
We know our love will never depart.

Day After

We said yes to this special wedding day.
Even if its an Internet cyber way.
All Our friends and the ones we care about were invited.
When they sent the responds back they were very excited.
A wedding is so complicated.
And now look, the day is here and we all have made it.
After we said I do we bonded together.
And now you're my wife forever.
I knew this love could never break us apart.
Cause yesterday I gave you my whole soul and heart.

To The One I Love!

I'll miss you because your not here.
And I know you don't live so near.
I'll wait I won't run away.
I love you forever and a day.
Cause you're my life.
I want you to be my wife.
You're my stars my sun and my moon.
I hope to be with you real soon.
My life without you would be so blue.
I can't live! Not even a day without you.
You're my food that feeds me every day.
Also the air that I breathe cause it helps me on my way.
You're my water that keeps me alive.
See without you I couldn't survive.
So baby listen I don't lie.
You're the apple of my eye.
So please remember the vows that we've taking.
I also promised you I'd never let your heart break; I know I'm not
mistaken.
So I let you take complete control.
Cause I've given you my heart my body and soul.

Yahoo

There's a room in yahoo chat where I been for a few days.
I'm a straight guy yet I'm chatting in a room that's called both ways.
I'm talking to my friends.
From the morning till the day ends.
I talk to people out of London and the USA.
Some are bad some are okay.
We play music in the room.
The beat goes then boom, boom, and boom.
And when people give us a hard time and a bad mood.
We had to try to settle them down because they're rude.
And don't cross the mic and throw a fit.
People will be furious and you're not going to like it.
When you're nice you're welcome in the room.
Enjoy yourself and when you have a good time we hope to see you
back very soon.

Hold On

I'm dreaming that I'm there.
I can see my hands going through your hair.
Our lips come together.
Girl I love you forever.
I can't let you go.
Baby I love you so.
Time is near.
And I don't fear.
Can't wait for the first time when we meet.
Oh my God it will be so neat.

Lovingyou.com

Every time I write a poem and put it on your site.
I write poetry in the morning also at night.
Most poems that I write are written about love.
And the Lord gives me words from above.
This site is very great.
And sometimes I can't wait.
The Lord gives me new words to write.
So I can show my love on this newfound website.
People you may mail me.
Your opinions are free.
You like the poems or not.
The opinion means to me a lot.
So people all you have to do.
Is to be honest and true.
So that's why I say thanks to this site so very much.
Every poem you'll read gives your heart a special touch.

For My Lover's Valentine

With this valentine card with beautiful art.
I give you the rest of my heart.
You're the one.
You're my rain and my sun.
I want to be close together with you.
This is what I really want to do.
It's like sharing my beautiful thoughts and mind.
Cause you are so nice and kind.
You taste like sugar just so sweet.
Can't wait for the day that we'll meet.
This card will let you see.
You're the only one for me.
You know all those words are from my heart.
That's why I send you this card; it could be the beginning of a new start.

Your Eyes

Every time I look in your eyes it's like a flame.
When I'm not with you I go insane.
I love you and that flame starts to become a fire.
I love you forever with all my desire.
I can't stop the love you give to me.
Your love is the best and with our son we're a family.
I'll never stop loving you.
And that is honestly true.
I'll never forget November 14th our special day.
Soon we're together in real that's all I pray.

Bad Day

At this moment I'm not f.i.n.e fine.
I feel hot and chills are running up and down my spine.
Can't bear this life with all the interfering.
Someone wants us apart cause I know people are trying.
Why do we have troubles in our life this way?
I thought everything was just Á okay.
Now there is pain and I don't have it under control.
You got all of me even my soul.
So take me as I am I'll be truthful you'll see.
I love you from now till eternity.
I can't live without you.
Don't know what else to do.
Soon we'll live our lives together.
From that day it will be forever.
No matter what the new day will bring.
I'll keep on doing my love thing.
I'll never run away.
You know I'll always stay.
No matter what happens in the end.
We're strong together as where we stand.

Till The Snow Is Gone

Today the snow was coming down.
There was a rainbow touching the ground.
We've seen stars shining so bright yesterday.
We where amazed when we found the Milky Way.
We never had seen this heavenly light.
It was such a beautiful sight.
The sun keeps on shining all day long.
Then the snow was eventually gone.
Until winter is all over I'll hold you endlessly.
I'm going to pull my love closer to me.
She gives me the warmth that I need.
She is everything yes indeed.
She keeps me warm like a sweater.
Cause we don't like this cold and bitter weather.
Baby will you please come and sit by me at this fire.
I need you and you're my only hearts desire.

A Memory Of November14th

Baby I know you'll remember.
The 14th of November.
The day we said "I do".
Yes it was on the Internet and it was pretty cool to.
I'll never forget that day.
It was the word yes I heard you say.
Everyone cried in the room.
You're now my bride and I'm your groom.
A poem for our vows, the words came from our heart.
Now I'm yours, and God knows we'll never depart.
People were at my bride's house.
Yet they were so quiet as a mouse.
Even the priest was in tears.
Now we're bond together I have no fears.
Every 14th of the month I'll let you remember.
That special night we shared in November.

Cloud Nine

I love the smile on your face.
I miss you when I don't see you through out the days.
When I gaze into your eyes.
Baby every day you make me fantasize.
The affection I feel from your love.
It brings me to cloud nine above.
Wish I could be with you right away.
I don't want to miss a freaking day.
My love grows.
I know it shows.
I know I dream of you every day.
I'll be there forever and I'll stay.
Our dreams will come true.
Cause my heart belongs only to you.
Time will tell when I come your way.
You and I both know we get along great every day.

Fell In Love With A Bbw

I saw the face of you.
And I knew.
I love the way you are.
I know you live in the USA and that's pretty far.
I Love your insides as well as your out.
Damn I feel proud! I just want to scream and shout.
The way you love me is so unreal.
I was hurt yet your love helped me to heal.
I know I doubted you in the beginning.
But our love is strong that's why we're winning.
Today I understand bbw's and how they're feeling inside.
When they love someone their love is endlessly and full of pride.
Their insides are so great like you.
I'm never going to doubt that's so true.
Come in my arms and hold me tight.
I'm so in love with you, and I need you tonight.

So Far Away

Why is it so hard! When your love one is so far away?
You wish you could be there like yesterday.
I need you in my arms to hold.
Until were both gray and old.
Never had love so strong like this.
I can even feel a touch of your kiss.
I'll never throw it away.
I'm here baby and I'll stay.
Some days I'm upset and you know.
I don't have to tell you my eyes will show.
I dislike this feeling deep inside.
These feelings! I just want to hide.
I can't bear to be alone.
I need your voice on the phone.
So it feels like you are close to me.
Baby I love you endlessly.
I married you the 14th of November.
A day I'll always remember.
Sweet as heaven is your kiss.
It's your presents that I miss.
I need your smile every day.
Oh my God you know I'll pray.
Soon we're close together.
It will be for Always and forever.

Lucky One

I'm a lucky guy.
And when you ask me why.
I will say.
My lover loves me this way.
She doesn't care.
She wants me there.
And the feeling is the same.
I love her, and even her name.
She gives me love like I never knew.
And I give it back everyday brand new.
It's not only her love that I won.
It's also the heart of her son.
That little guy said already.
Massy you're my daddy.

You And I

To my baby I love you so.
I hate it when you have to go.
I miss you so bad.
It makes me always sad.
I long to hear your voice in my ears.
I hope for many of years.
You're the one that brightens my day.
Yes it was you that showed me the way.
I long to be with you through out my whole life.
That's why I pray to God that you want to be my wife.
I look to the Lord up above.
Please keep us together with your love.

Time

Time ticks away.
And every night I pray.
I'll see you soon, before the end of time.
I know your love is the same just like mine.
Every night on the Internet we meet.
When I hear your voice my heart starts to beat.
Girl I love the words you say to me.
I can talk to you endlessly.
From your words I make poems very fast.
After time the poems will forever last.
So give me new words and songs to write.
It kills the time for me tonight.

No One Else

I see a light when I close my eyes.
My girl is beautiful and hides in disguise.
Yet she brings fire to my soul.
Her love makes my life whole.
For me she takes off her mask.
She said to me it was not an easy task.
No one else saw her like this.
She makes me shiver when I gave her that first kiss.
She is my light my strength my beacon of hope.
We went under the shower and I rubbed her with soap.
She's all I want and need; she's more then I expected in life.
She's going to be the perfect wife.
There will be no one else in my life any more.
I found a lady who understands me better then anyone before.
Soon we'll get married and be together.
I know it will be great, a lifetime with her forever.

Love Of My Life

You're so true I know this, because God sent you.
You make me happy, so I don't feel blue.
Our love that we share is so fresh as the rain.
And your hands take away my pain.
Just the way it should.
Girl your love is so good.
Baby I know you, yes I can see.
It's pure love between you and me.
Your songs make my heart sing.
And I wear your wedding ring.
We share a love that can't compare.
To anyone else and nowhere.
You and I will live our lives together and have fun.
God put us together to be as one.

My Son

Little sport you're my son, and your love for me is very strong.
Love to see your smile on your face all day long.
The expression I can see in your eyes.
Gives me a loving surprise.
You're a perfect son.
It's my heart you won.
You miss me when I'm not home.
Wish I were there so you don't feel alone.
When I come home we'll go to a park.
Playing till it gets dark.
So we'll have lots of fun.
God I love you my son.

Forest Walk

Walking through the woods for hours.
It's summer and we smell all the beautiful flowers.
We heard the birds chirping their song.
We follow a path along.
We have just so much fun.
You looked to me and to our little son.
Playing hide and seek.
Follow the road down by creek.
Some deer's are passing by.
You feel so happy that you started cry.
And when we're home I make dinner for three.
Cause my love for my family is endlessly.

Beach

Walking on the beach side by side at night.
The water is touched by moonlight so bright.
You see champagne on ice.
And candles around a blanket so nice.
We made love because our love never stops.
Then I'm going to hold you till the sun drops.
I love you every day.
That's what I want to say.
Come lay in my arms so you'll never go.
Can't stop to telling you; baby I love you so.

I Asked You First

I want to live my life with you.
Forever and ever I tell you this is true.
You said you want to marry me.
One day I'll make that dream come true you'll see.
Because you know I want to marry you.
I asked you first and you said; "Yes I do".
You asked me yesterday would you marry me baby.
I said why not you make me love crazy.
You know I will, because your love gives me a thrill.
Your heart for me will never sit still.
When our lives join together as one.
Oh my God baby we'll have so much fun.
You and I and our little son are a family.
We'll all live together happily.

Letter To My Son

Here's a letter to my son.
I love you all day long my little one.
This life with you is my life I feel it already.
I know you feel it to because you call me daddy.
You're already my son for real.
You know that's the way I really feel.
I never understood why you listen to me.
I'm going to be the best daddy for you you'll see.
We'll all have fun in our life.
May I marry your mommy and make her my wife?
I'll never hurt your little heart.
Nor will I ever depart.
You and your mommy mean everything to me.
When I go to heaven, I'll be there as an angel to protect you for
eternity.

Spring

Spring is coming very soon.
Can you see the bright moon?
It's very nice outside.
The moon draws to the tide.
You're sitting in my arms tonight.
Yes I hold you very tight.
We're making love while the rain gets us dripping wet.
A nice moment you and I should never forget.
Bodies started to sweat when we touch each other.
Even the rain won't let us stop or even give us a bother.
Making love outside in the rain I never did that before.
Don't stop the love making let me take you once more.
We screamed while we both exploded together as one.
We're going to make love till the rising of the sun.

Words In My Agenda

I met this girl at my school.
She is awesome and very cool.
She wrote some words just for me.
Read a little bit further and you'll see.

(In my agenda she put these words.)

Life is not easy and it never will be.
You have your friends and one of them of course is me.
So when your in trouble, and don't know what to do.
Just call my name because I believe in you.

Nicole thanks you very much.
Your words reached my heart with a nice touch.
It will always be a part of my heart.
And it means to me a lot right from the start.
It gives the meaning of friendship, which will never end.
So for that I'll thank you my friend.

By The Sea

We are lying by the sea.
We're hugging and kissing just you and me.
We felt the water coming over us.
As we make love not lust.
While we watch the sun slowly going down.
I caress your body with my hands all around.
I feel your body pressing against mine.
Baby you're skin is soft it feels so warm and fine.
This is the best; we make love slowly not to fast.
I want this love forever to last.
I'll light up some candles when the moon starts to rise.
The love we make feels like a tropical paradise.
Let me kiss and tease your body everywhere.
I know every time we make love its so amazing, the climax we
share.
Making love on the beach while the sun starts to drop.
We're making love when you're climbing on top.
And when we climax together its like an explosion.
I say: baby I love you forever, and I'll show you all of my devotion.

Beat Of The Heart

Every day goes by and I'll never regret.
Remembering how we met on the Internet.
One year ago.
I can't let the feeling go.
You give me your love, and I gave you mine.
We'll stay together till the end of time.
I'll stomped my feet.
To every heart beat.
And say baby come here kiss my lips.
Touch my face with your fingertips.
We finely touch skin to skin.
And we'll never let anyone else in.
With every heartbeat, it beats your name.
Without you my world wouldn't be the same.

Freedom

There's this feeling inside.
I can't show it I have to hide.
I've done this for a very long while.
Hiding away was just my style.
I couldn't act like who I wanted to be.
But now I met someone who set me free.
With no worries in my life I feel better today.
God answered my prayers in a special way.
Now I'm back like the person I was before.
Silly and serious you couldn't ask for more.
Maybe With a little twist! Of romance and love.
I thank God for my girlfriend; she's an angel from above.
She likes the way I talk and everything I do.
I heard her say: my heart flutters; it makes me want to sing for you.
When we met she said; baby please never let me go.
I will never! Cause baby I love you so.

Champagne On Ice

I want to take you from behind.
Because that thought is now on my mind.
This is love that we share.
I know It, cause I can feel it I'm there.
I'll take you nice and slow, so very gently.
Love the way you moan and groan with me.
When you move up and down, there's a feeling I can't hide.
God I want to be with you and inside.
I love the way you move, cause it's so sensational.
You give your love unconditional.
We drink champagne on ice.
Cause tonight baby, it will be so nice.

My Family

To my family that's so close in my heart.
Here some words to the ones I love the most before I depart.
I'm going to leave this place for more then just a little while.
So I'll give you a number for you to dial.
When you feel alone.
Call me on the phone.
My family you'll be always in my heart.
You know this from the start.
No matter what will happen, Willo you're my best friend.
I'll love you till the end.
My family I never want to lose you and I won't lie.
But I know this for sure, without my girl I will die.
I'll try to come home on a vacation! Will that do?
My family and friends let me say this before I go, (I'LL AWAYS
LOVE YOU.)

To My Family In The Netherlands

My family is very important to me.
And I thought by myself, I want to break free.
There's a love at a distance, she loves me the way I'm inside.
I realize love has no boundaries there's no reason to hide.
Some people say loving some one at a distance could never be.
Yet love will brings us together you'll see.
Since I've met her, my life has changed forever.
Whether we're apart or together.
I feel her close in my heart.
I'll promise to be there and never depart.
For as long as I live, I'll stand by her side.
I'll always be close by like the moon draws the tide.
I'm just a phone call away for you.
Pick up the phone is all you need to do.
Our door will always be open for you all.
No matter if it's during the day or at nightfall.
Just know we'll never turn away.
You're all a part of my heart and there you'll stay.
And then I'm going to say.
I love my family forever and a day.

From Candy To Werner's Family

This is to my boyfriend's family; I love him with all my heart.
So please don't push or shove cause you'll tear us apart.
You all know that I'm in love.
With your son, that God has sent to me from above.
Let me love your son like you do.
Let us all stay happy, and not blue.
Enjoy our new life, which we choose for eternity.
Cause in his heart you'll always be.
Remember love ones you'll never lose our connection.
All you have to do is fly in our direction.
I know your son is very important to you all.
Just Pick up the phone or maybe we'll even give you call.
As your son and I join hands, we'll stand together.
My son and I can't wait to be with your son forever.
We want you all to know, to us you're important to.
I want you all to accept us to your family, like we will you.

Fantasy In A Shop

My girl and I were in a dressing room where we where shopping.
I made love with her very slow; there was no way of stopping.
We where spotted yet we didn't care.
I wanted to make love with her right there.
She was sitting on her knees.
It's so amazing the way she knew how to tease.
Then we switched places, caressing her body was just a start.
When I lowered down I played with her ring in her privet part.
I asked her to bend over for me.
While making love I whispered in her ear; I love you endlessly.
Our bodies where moving nice and slow.
We wished that this moment would never go.
Her climax reached the top, moaning and groaning she came that
night
She let her juices flow while I was holding her tight.
I want to stay with her the rest of my life.
She's my lover and soon to be my wife.

Cheating

Why do you think people cheat?
Don't they get the love (sex) they need?
A relationship is built on love, honesty and trust.
Not on sex or lust.
When you lay down with some one other then your partner that's
bad.
Then don't be surprise when your partner is mad.
Why cheat and lie, when you have a good partner next to you?
When you know a good partner is hard to find, and you know this
is true.
I'm in love with the most beautiful woman a man can wish for.
I don't have the desire to lie down and kiss another no more.
I heard when you cheat your heart will feel guilty in the end.
So I know I'll never cheat cause I want to stay worthy to my girl
friend.
Lust makes a person have a guilty feeling inside.
It only lowers the person that you are, and it doesn't do much for
your pride.
So start you life with trust, honesty and love.
Than the Lord will help you from heaven above.

This Is To My MASSY

You're the daddy that I love.
Your love is a gift sent from heaven above.
I promise I'll try to listen closely to you.
Massy I love you, and my mommy feels the same way to.
From the day we met you, we felt the pokies in your touch.
We let you come into our hearts, cause Massy we love you so
much.
Massy when are you coming home?
Cause mommy and I don't like to be alone.
I'll be your son forever.
Then we'll stay as a family together.
Massy I love you every day.
I'll pray you'll come soon okay.
Massy I want you to come here right now.
Cause I'll say in Dutch (I love you) ik hou van jou.

When It Rains

The rain is falling down on the ground.
It's also ticking against our window, baby can you hear the sound?
But baby! I don't want to wake up to a rainy day.
Please God let the rain stop, or chase the clouds away.
Today is our day off so lets stay in bed to rest.
I can feel my girl friends hands and her head on my chest.
Nice and warm we're both under the sheet.
I'll Snuggle close, cause I want to hear her heart beat.
When we get up from bed, I'll make coffee for two.
Cause darling that is what I want to do for you.

Thoughts From My Girl
(When He Comes)

When my boyfriend comes to the USA.
I hope he'll want to stay.
Every night I pray when I go to bed.
His voice is resounding in my head.
I know he'll like it here with me.
He told me; if I could I'd move for you the mountains and the sea.
He speaks very well English and it's so cool.
He did it by himself, cause he never learned it at school.
I want him to give us a chance.
When he comes here we can all dance.
I want to make it a special place for us two.
He and I will get married and be true.
When he steps off that plane he'll see.
The USA is a place for him to be.
When our eyes meet, my heart will start to beat very fast.
He said; come here baby and kiss me forever last.

I Want Her To Know

Her smile drives me wild.
She's so innocence as a little child.
I like that in her it's a nice style.
I said, Come over here and sit with me for a little while.
Then she said; come on lets walk by the trees.
Lets go out and feel the nice soft breeze.
She set down on a bench near me.
She whispered in my ear; you fulfill me so completely.
I'm so into her, I really don't see the people, who are walking by.
I don't hear a thing, not even the birds singing in the sky.
I'm so lost in love when I look in her eyes.
She takes me to a newfound paradise.
My body floats whenever she's around.
I can't even put my feet back on the ground.
So now you see what her love does to me.
I told her yesterday, baby I love you for eternity.
She sets my body and soul on fire.
She's my one and only hearts desire.

She Went On A Visit To A New Place

She couldn't believe the man she met on her journey.
He was as gentle as a man could be.
When he turned around and took a look at her.
Her heart melted that's for sure.
She felt butterflies and started to giggle right away.
He walked right up to her that memorable Day.
Her face was turning very red.
She didn't run away, she said hi instead.
He said; I've seeing you about a year ago in November.
She replied, yes you have, it's amazing you still remember.
She spoke and said; I come from the USA, I needed a little break.
He replied; welcome to the Netherlands; it will be no mistake.
While he smiled at her, she said, I have to find a place to stay.
Well come on he said let me show you around okay.
He took her to this lovely place.
She loved the expression on his face.
They stayed together and had dinner that night.
He walked her to the hotel while the moon was shining so bright.
When he kissed her he said, I'll pick you up tomorrow at seven.
She couldn't believe he's back in her life, it felt like she was in
heaven.
He said; I'll see you tomorrow as he walked away.
Because he had to go She said with a little sorrow, okay.

Just A Touch

When I think of you, I can feel your touch.
Baby I love you so very much.
All I do is pray.
When I come to you, I want to stay.
Now you know why English is my goal.
USA you took my heart and soul.
My girl friend lives in the USA.
I want to be with her, cause I miss her every day.
That's why I pack my bags and take the first flight.
I know she love me as much as I love her, cause she cry's every night.
Few hours to fly and I'm there where I belong.
I know what I'm doing, my heart told me this, and I know it's not wrong.
Baby I would love to take you as my bride.
I'll stand forever by you side.
And this is what I want to do.
Cause no one can stop me from loving you.
Baby let's go elope today.
Because I love you so much my heart will never stray away.

Tired

I woke up this morning feeling like I needed more sleep.
I didn't sleep much, yet I slept to deep.
My wife said; he sleepy head good morning.
I open my eyes and said; I love you darling.
Hey! You're already to late for work today.
No time for breakfast your plate will have to stay.
I said to wife coffee is all I need this morning.
Just as I started to leave, the phone starts ringing.
It was my boss yelling to me that I was an hour to late
I rushed around this morning and it didn't start great.
I asked my boss to give me an hour and I'll be fine.
I guess my boss and I partied to late and now I'm not worth a dime.

Never Leave Me

How many men would stay?
After what you did that day.
I proved it to you by wearing you ring.
Doesn't that mean a thing?
You know I love your son like my own child.
It doesn't matter if he's nice or a little wild.
Please never say you want to have a break from me.
Because I know my heart won't take it, can't you see?
You know my love for you is strong.
What I felt wasn't wrong.
I don't need any time away from you.
I need you in my life, so please stay that's all you need to do.
Why give up something so perfect between you and I.
You know if we did we would both sit and cry.
I can't live a day without you no more.
It would kill me! I never loved some one like this before.
So never ask me to take time apart.
I knew I loved you from the start.
I love you forever and a day.
You promise me you would stay.
The words you said are still in my mind.
I love you so much my love for you is blind.

I Love You So Much

Hi, I just wanted to write.
I've been up all night.
I can't sleep or get any rest.
My heart is beating for you so fast.
More then words, is all we have to say.
Take my hand and lets run away.
Into the sunset you'll find.
That I was waiting there for you all the time.
Come my love and take me away.
I want to live with you every night and day.
You're my true love in my heart and soul.
Without you baby I wouldn't be whole.
I love you so much, and that's no lie.
Cause for me you're an angel that fell from the sky.

Massy And I

Massy and I love mommy very much.
Mommy and I speak English and Massy is teaching us Dutch.
With my sister there is three.
When Massy comes here it makes four, like a family.
I loved Massy from start.
I took his love in my heart.
And that's where our friendship began.
Mommy said; she loves this man.
No matter what the future will bring us tomorrow.
The Lord will show us a life without any sorrow.
I cherish the feelings that we share.
From the moment we met there will be no despair.
Mommy, sissy and I love you for eternity.
We take you Massy as a part of our family.

Lovemaking In The Pool

Our bodies where hot and the water was cool.
We made love last night in our swimming pool.
She kissed me softly with her smooth sweet lips.
Then she touched my rod with her fingertips.
Stroking it very slow and nice.
I told her damn you sent me to paradise.
My fingers stroking her privet part deep inside.
I lifted her up to set her on me for a wild ride.
When I penetrate her deep within.
My hands where caressing her skin.
Then she turned and said; take me from behind.
Don't move slow move please fast if you don't mind.
She screamed and hollers for more.
This love is the best that I ever felt before.
I kissed her with my tongue.
With a desire of a fire ignites, and very long.
Together we end in ecstasy.
This love is better than any fantasy.

Lovers Eternal Flame

Destiny is only a door.
Open it and you will find me for evermore.
I'm waiting with open arms and wanting you to hold.
Loves tender hug pressed our bodies together like silver and gold.
Holds me close while my love tingles through our kiss it makes
me insane.
Passions burning inside like an eternal flame.
It is like a fire that's makes my love so passionate.
I'll caress your body with my hands cause you're my soul mate.
My love burns only for you.
I love you every day brand new.
Let are love devour in uncontrolled passion tonight.
In this world and beyond I'll hold you tight.
Reaching the ultimate climax until the world melts away.
And forever we'll be together and stay.
I know you feel the same.
We're in love with a lover's eternal flame.

Passion And Desire

I have this craving desire.
It heats me up and brings out the fire.
You walked to me and made my heart beat.
I'm sweating from my head till my feet.
The desire in me sets up like a flame.
I know it's you! You're the blame.
You touch your self while you strip.
I can't handle this erotic wild trip.
I want to make love with you baby.
Seeing your body makes me wild and crazy.
Don't just shake your nice tight booty to me.
Come here and fast yet do it smoothly.
Make love with me and please don't stop.
Ride me like an animal when you sit on top.
Your lovemaking is breathtaking.
There's no way of mistaking.
Baby my love will be only for you.
You're a dream that just came true.
Our heart beats so fast as a train.
My love will last forever like a pouring rain.
Come make love to me and you'll see.
My love for you is wild and for eternity.

I Love You

I love you for the person you are from the inside.
Not for what you look like on the outside.
Nor the clothes you wear.
Or the money you have I don't care.
You are perfect as you are.
Just like a bright shining star.
My heart is not made of stone.
I wont ever leave you alone.
I love you for who you are inside.
God may be a witness and my guide.
I know you feel the same way for me.
Cause your love is unconditionally.
You're my lover and soon to be my wife.
You'll be forever a big part of my life.
I'll love you just the way you are for evermore.
It really doesn't matter if you're rich or poor.
No one can change my mind.
Because you where already hard to find.
Now that I have you I'll never let you walk away.
Cause we love each other forever and a day.

Night's Passion

There's a sound that trembles in my soul.
It takes over all my control.
I feel it in my head and in my heart.
You whisper my name like fine art.
Like a lover's passion touch deep into the night.
Falling stars are crossing the sky, when my heart takes a flight.
I'll make your desires reality.
I'll bring you into total ecstasy.
Our sweaty bodies will touch as we lay side by side.
The heat rises and I have erotic feelings that I cant hide.
So when you touch me in my secret place.
I feel tingles in my neck my belly and even on my face.
Our excitement grew stronger while I caressed your skin.
A passionate kiss leads me to a journey deep within.
We climaxed till we both were out of breath that night.
Baby your love making drives me insane but that's all right.
Together we lay to cool down after our night of passion.
I wrap my arms around you cause I'm old fashion.
It's for real this love I carry for you.
My love is unconditional and forever true.

Finally We Met

You're my moon and I'm your star.
Why do we have to live so far?
Love reaches in our souls and in our heart.
We're in love yet not so far Apart.
You're my Juliet that willing to die.
God knows I love you all I do is cry.
When you're surrounded by gloom.
Just remember your Romeo is waiting for you to come home soon.
Swim across the ocean, fly across the sea.
I'll be there with arms wide open just wait and see.
Then I'll open the door.
When you come in you don't have to leave no more.
Come sit down with me and have a cup of hot tea.
Your time here will be so happy and free.
When I ask you; will you marry me today?
So we'll live here happy together, forever and a day.
I turned around and she gave me a smile.
She said; I've been waiting for you to say this for a long while.

Wanting

I set by the phone to hear your voice.
I wait for the mail its my second choice.
Of course the Internet is where we first met.
I love you so much you make my body sweat.
I'll cuddle you and caress you and kiss your lips.
While you slide your hands down my hips.
Your passion goes through my mind like a flame of fire.
You turn me on with an erotic desire.
I'll kiss you and caress your body all up and down.
Then I turn your body completely around.
Even we switch from bottom to top.
I moan and scream baby please don't stop.
Her nails dragged down my chest.
When the rhythm aroused she was on her best.
A little bit later she climaxed like she never did before.
She said; I love you so much, yet I want you once more.

Today Is Not A Good Day

I don't feel very swell.
My tummy is not so well.
I really want to be with you.
But I'm sick and I have the flu.
Sleeping is all that I need when I'm sick.
It's hard to wake me up because I sleep like a Brick.
I don't like to be sick, that's why I'm upset and mad.
So when people stay away it makes me glad.
I want to tell them I'm sick and I need some space.
When I'm feeling better I'll call them in a few days.
Still there are people walking in and out.
With their kids they still let them scream and shout.
The kids don't care that I'm sick.
God! I'd love to give them a kick.
It's real hard for my son and I to get better.
It's because all this changing in the Weather.
We've been quite sick for a long time.
We drink orange juice with a bit of lime.
I really don't want my boy friend to be alone.
So I called him for a moment on the phone.
I said to him; sorry we've not been together because I have the flu.
He replied back to me; it doesn't matter baby I still love you.
He said; I'll come to you when you are better.
Maybe the three of us can go to the zoo to have fun all together.

Day Dreaming

I had this dream in my head last night.
It was about my girlfriend dressed in white.
She was waiting at the altar for me.
When you saw her face she looked so happy.
I love this woman just the way she is.
I feel every expression in her kiss.
It's hard for me to even gasp for air.
I don't know if she realizes she looks beautiful with that hair.
You are my woman and I love you in every way.
I want you to know I need you every night and day.
I'll never let you go out of my life.
Cause in my dream you became my wife.
I gave you my heart my body and my soul with this ring.
My friends know, to me you're everything.
I'll love this woman till the end of time.
Loving her so much isn't a crime
They all agree and said we're cute.
See baby I love you there's no dispute.

First Day Of Our Little Boy

Seeing our little boy go to school.
He looks happy and his clothes are cool.
To bad we couldn't be there.
Sometimes life isn't fair.
We where crying for him cause he's growing up so fast.
Yet we can't live in the past.
Hopefully he had a great day.
We missed him more than we could say.
Its weird he's going to be gone for an hour or three.
The house is now so silent for my wife and me.
We miss his cute little face and voice.
Now we can't even enjoy when he's playing with his toys.
It will be a daily thing that he will be going away.
God now we're going to feel so alone every day.
The hours pass by slowly and it drives us crazy.
All we thought about was our baby.
Then we heard the bus and our little boy walk through the door.
He came to us and dropped his backpack on to the floor.
He was talking so fast.
We felt so happy he said school was a blast.
We missed him so much when he was away.
And it will be like this when he's at school every day.

This Is What I'm Going To Do

I'm going to end the love that I'm with.
And be with you and start a new relationship.
I'm going to leave her for you.
This is what I'm going to do.
How must I tell her how I feel inside?
I love you and I can't hide.
We started as friends.
But now we're lovers till the end.
You showed me what love is all about.
This is God's work I have no doubt.
From the moment I met you.
I was in love I already knew.
I never felt like this before.
Now I love you each day more and more.
I'm going to start a new life with you.
Every bump in the road we'll pull through.
Never doubt my love for you.
I'm leaving my girlfriend this is what I want to do.
We'll find happiness together.
From today and forever.
Till the day we die.
I'll stand by your side.

Mystery

It's a mystery.
That a girl like you could love a guy like me.
God knew that I couldn't let you go.
Cause I love you very much so.
Five lonely years went by.
And this is no lie.
I dreamed and looked for you everywhere.
Suddenly! You were there.
We spend hours together on the Internet.
And I have no regret.
I had to wait a long time.
Now we're back together and it feels fine.
The love that we share is beyond this place.
I'll tell you the waiting will be no waist.
My love is pure like gold in my heart.
That's why I can't leave you or my world will fall apart.

Life

I'm walking away from all the troubles and the pain.
I'm crying while I'm walking through the rain.
Lots of people made me mad and angry today.
I feel lost and I see my life fading away.
I don't want to live this way no more.
I'm planning to die today that's for sure.
It's enough that people are hurting me.
I'm better off in heaven where I can live free.
I had a bad thought in my mind.
Is it wise to leave my beloved family behind?
I was walking with a lot of things going through my brain.
Like jumping off a building or should I throw myself in front of a
train?
I decide to end my life.
Just by cutting my wrist with a knife.
I have seen blood everywhere.
I opened my eyes, I didn't see heaven, but I the seen intensive care.
What was the reason that I didn't die?
I asked God! I'm still alive, why?
He said you have to do something for me.
You must write with your heart some poetry.
It will touch the hearts of millions of people in the world some day.
So that's the reason you live but I will help you on your way.
Here I am writing poetry as the Lord asks me that night.
Ending your life just isn't right.
Giving up your life isn't God's way; it's evil that likes to play.
Follow me to a better place said God; or evil gets his way.

I Feel The Same

A beautiful woman walked down the street pretty fast.
It was the same woman that I met in my past.
She still looks the same.
Memories of her came back into my brain.
I ran after her and asked, do you remember me?
We met on your vacation! On that Dutch riverboat sailing to the sea!
That boat trip sailed to Budapest it was a blast.
When I saw you my heart was beaten fast.
She said; oh my God it's you! I remember you so how are you these days?
I'm great I said; do you like coffee? I always go to this neat little place.
She said I'd love to, so we went to the café for a cup of coffee.
Then suddenly she told me; how much she really loves me.
I was amazed! And I said I feel the same.
I introduce my self and Candice was her name.
I showed her a poem that I kept for years.
When she read it she busted into tears.
She said God I wish you could come home to my son and I and build a home.
Cause Werner you fulfill my heart with your words in your poem.
I said you sure! That you want to do this?
Then she gave me a passionate kiss.
She said; if I could marry you today I would gladly say yes I do.
Cause for a lot of years I have been in love with you.

True Love

When I looked to the stars in the sky above.
I prayed to God for a special love.
How can I find the love inside of me?
Can you find love on the first sight that last for eternally?
In my youth I worked on a boat and I had seen a beautiful face.
My heart was pounding with a feeling I never could erase.
Was this true love I felt that day?
Cause the feeling was weird yet great in a way.
Is this true? Am I in love with this lady?
I really don't know but I would say maybe.
Last thing I remember was seeing her leaving the boat and
walking on the shore.
From that moment I felt sad more then before.
I picked up my life but I had a feeling something inside wasn't right.
There was never that same feeling as on the boat on that special
night.
I had dates and even a relationship for over a year maybe three.
Yet I couldn't find the right one for me.
I was in the chat room one night on the Internet.
There I met a girl and I had an old feeling while we're in a privet
chat.
With an amazing shock it was the same girl I met a few years back
in my life.
At this moment we're tight together as man and wife.

Red Light

I went into Amsterdam to this erotic place.
There lays a memory of a beautiful face.
I was walking on this very small street.
There she was little bit heavy but oh so sweet.
They call it the red light district in the Netherlands that is what people told me.
I never have been there in my life before but I heard it's a place to be.
It was just for fun to walk down this exotic place.
Suddenly it was pouring rain onto my face.
That heavy lady called me into her room because of the rain.
I told her I'll stay till the rain is over cause sex wasn't in my brain.
I know I taken her time so I gave her the money cause I felt bad with this.
We talked for a bit then with a surprise she lift up my chin for a passionate kiss.
The feeling she gave me I couldn't hide.
I touch her skin we laid down on our side.
It felt like I was on cloud nine above.
It felt so good I didn't call it sex; we made passionate love.
Few hours later it wasn't raining any more.
I thanked and kiss her before I walked out of her door.
It's so funny like I knew her from the past and what I seen in her eyes.
It felt strange and I walked away yet I felt I was in paradise.

The Reason

When you asked me how deep is your love.
Then I would say as much as there're stars in the sky above.
I'll cry when I'm not with you.
You know that my love for you is like gold and not blue.
I never let you get out of my sight.
I'll protect you without even having to fight.
You're like a flower that blooms in the spring.
I feel your love that you carry deep within.
You're like a warm summer rain.
When I see you my heart goes fast like a train.
Never seen a girl that has eyes as blue as the sea.
Girl I love you endlessly.
Your touch makes me every time shake.
There's no way our love would ever break.
Your lips are so sweet like honey.
You make my darker days beautiful and sunny.
I feel blessed that I have you in my life forever and more.
You and our son make that perfect family that I adore.
Girl I love you for eternity.
And the reason we'll never break is because you're in love with me.

Depression

When people say you do everything wrong.
It will make you slowly weak and not very strong.
You'll walk with a frown cause there's no reason for a smile on
your face.
It can happen to everybody and at any place.
When you lost everything you adore.
Don't sit and cry on the floor.
When you start to believe nothing is going your way.
Or wondering is God listening when I pray?
Mean people are always saying you do nothing right.
I know it makes you think all through the night.
Start by not listening to what those people have said.
Just stand up and get the worries out of your head.
Coming out a depression is hard to do.
You could ask friends and family to see if they maybe could help
you.
Society does it all I know it for sure.
Just look inside of yourself there you find the cure.
People that put you down are more insecure then you think.
They want to have power to see how fast and low you will sink.
You have to learn to stand up and be someone.
My vision is, to fight against depression with laughter, humor and
fun.

Hope

Five years ago a girl was hoping to find me back in her life.
There were some days she lost hope, and she thought, he's already taken a wife.
Five years back I gave my heart to a girl without a clue.
Cause she never told me where she lived, finding her back was hard to do.
I put the memories of her far back in my mind.
Cause I knew she was hard to find.
She married and divorced a guy.
And I was with a girl! I won't lie.
Our relationship with our partners was very bad.
We both wished for that person from our past, because we didn't lose the feelings we had.
On the Internet I found the girl of my past back with a surprise.
That girl recognized me by looking into my eyes.
She didn't tell this in the beginning cause I had to feel the love deep within.
God knew what she was doing so it wasn't a sin.
I asked her; do I know you? Cause it seems I heard your voice before.
Seems I wasn't so sure I'd paid no attention on it any more.
My ex was getting jealous, yet there was nothing that I could do.
In the meantime! My love grew stronger for that girl on the Internet, that's so true.
I had to make a very hard decision in my life.
So I said goodbye to my ex, and the girl on the Internet is now my wife.

Two Weeks

A dream came true.
Finally two weeks with you.
Now you can make love with me.
We'll fulfill our erotic fantasy.
We've been waiting for this so very long.
The desire for making love is unbelievably strong.
There are scented candles burning so bright.
I'll make your vacation exciting every night.
In the background we hear the music play.
We're making love tonight till the following day.
I bought some champagne and put it on ice.
Pour a little on me and taste it from my skin, it will bring us both
to paradise.
Making love against your will, I never would do.
I want to make these two weeks special for you.
I love to see your body move.
Let us use toys only when you would approve.
Can't believe I'm lying by your side.
I'll kiss you tender and slowly we start on an erotic ride.
You're coming with a moan that brings us to cloud nine or even
higher.
This little flame burst into an eternal fire.
Girl I'm so glad you're the love of my life.
I know you can't wait to marry me so you can say; I'm his wife.

Teasing With A Devilish Plan

She pushed me on the bed.
She brought my hands above my head.
I had seen everywhere candlelight.
Then suddenly she locked my wrists in handcuffs but not to tight.
Very tender she kissed my lips.
While she touch my body with her fingertips.
She teases me so freaking much.
There's no way for me to reach out and touch.
She has a devilish plan in her mind.
She was using toys on my behind.
With her hands and her lips, she touched my manly hood.
What she done to me felt so good.
Our hearts beating quickly while our bodies heated up even more.
I knew she wouldn't stop; she just would tease me harder then
before.
She slows down and crawls up and kisses my trembling lips.
Her hands touched my legs; her nails were digging in my hips.
She said; I want you inside of me.
Cause I want to feel you explode of ecstasy.
She unlocked my hands and I reached out to run my nails on her
back.
With a passionate kiss I touched her lips and neck.
She set me on fire and I can't take the heat any more.
She lets me explode like I never exploded before.

Love For You

You're the love I have dreamed so long for.
I wished you only lived next door.
You brighten my world with many things.
Like a rainbow in the sky after it sings.
You cool me with a breeze on a summer day.
While we watch the children outside at play.
You fill my heart with so much love.
You're my angel sent to me from above.
You understand me better than most do.
You said its because you love me through and through.
I've never had someone like you.
You give me more than any other woman could ever do.
When I'm down your right there for me.
You hold me and tell me things will be good you'll see.
When I'm with you after a moment or two.
You said! See how much I love you cause my love is so true.
When I start to cry.
You're right there asking me, baby why?
Baby let me tell you this from the bottom of my heart.
I love you so much I know we'll never part.

Just To Say I Love You

Baby you're my miracle I had in my life.
Couldn't wait to marry you and make you my wife.
Our life was wonderful yet not forever.
In my heart I know we stay for an eternal life together.
A life without you I can't dream of.
I've been affected by a spell of love.
I'm dreaming now of you every night.
Lying next to you holding you tight.
Baby you're all that I need, and I don't wish for more.
My life is now better then it was before.
You're the one that found the key to my heart.
I'll come to you and never will we ever depart.
Honey I know you'll like this line that I'm about to say!
I'll love you forever and a day.
Yet I see you now as my angel up in the sky.
You looked down on me and I start to cry.
You didn't want to be there without my love.
Yet you'll hold for me a place in heaven above.
I loved you with all of my heart.
That's why it hurts, that we're now torn apart.
You're an angel now yet I'm here on earth.
I don't want you to see that I'm hurt.
I know it's not your fault that you're there.
Baby I miss you more then I even could bear.

A Little Possessive

These are some words I probably shouldn't write.
I'm making myself sad and that's a scary fright.
I'm in fear that when people talk to you during the day.
They're going to try to lead your heart away.
Sometimes I don't think right.
It makes me feel bad and twist and turn all night.
And that's not okay because I'm so in love with you.
Seems people can't even get the clue.
When I see them talking to you in a sexy way.
I set back and pray they don't lead your heart to stray.
I only hope my love I give to you is strong.
If someone tries to come between us it's wrong.
I'll fight for you till the end of time.
Just to let people know you're mine.
I know I'm jealous and a little possessive when it comes to you.
To keep you I'll fight or try whatever I can do.
So baby please understand my love is so strong and real.
I'll say it from my heart so you know how I feel.
I'll love you a lifetime if you let me.
You and I can be so happy just wait and see.

Body & Soul

When I look to you.
I see a female so true.
You have a heart full of love.
And a soul that's soft as a dove.
You always think of your mate.
You never have words of hate.
When people come to you.
And you see there down and blue.
You always try to make them smile.
Even though when it's just for a little while.
I see you as a perfect female like I never knew.
You take control and take a point of view.
You always say honey listen to me.
I'll help you in any way can't you see.
You're a female of good will and grace.
I can feel it through your hands when you touch my face.
So I'm here to say.
I love you in every way.
You have a heart and soul as pure as gold.
I just want it to be said and told.
I love you deeply and that's no lie.
Cause when you not here with me, all I want to do is cry.

I Ask For Nothing More

To My Beloved Girl Candice From Your Luck Master

The first time I fell in love was when I saw you.
God had sent you cause I prayed for two.
We only talked one special night, yet our hearts were beaten as one.
I started to miss you when you where gone.
For a long time you where out of my life.
I'll remember November 14th, it's the day you became my wife.
I'm so happy you're back, and I blessed that day.
We'll be together and I'll stay.
I'll not be complete without you.
My life would be so empty and blue.
There's no love better then yours that I can dream of.
I'll do everything to keep a hold of our love.
I never had feelings so deep for any one.
I don't only love you but also our son.
When I'm with you I feel so good.
I love you! I hope I say it enough like I should.
After you let me in when you opened your heart.
It's a beginning with a fresh new start.
Baby I love you with all my heart every day.
I'll love you till death takes us both away.
I'll pray for us forever.
That we'll be growing old together.

This poem was for our cyber Anniversary.

November 14th 2003.

If Only She Knew.

When I look deep in my heart.
I see a love that never will depart.
Strange love like this I never felt before.
It's because I lost her once but not any more.
The connection is very tight.
Cause this love is so right.
She's my lover I know this for sure.
For every sickness I have, she's my cure.
This girl is destined to be with me.
For her I give my love unconditionally.
So amazed when we found our love back after all those years.
A lifetime with her is perfect and I see no fears.
For me she's like a perfect flower.
I'd love to smell her each hour.
She's like a breeze of sweet fresh air.
That blows in my face and through my hair.
She's my rain on a sunny summer day.
With every drop she would wash my tears away.
If only she knew what her love means to me.
I can't say it with millions of words; it's just a feeling I'll keep for
eternity.

I Want Her Back!

I've been torn apart.
An angel broke my heart.
Reasons where running through my head.
I was hurt deep and very sad.
She walked out the door without a word to say.
I fell on my knees crying and I started to pray.
Oh God I thought this love was ment to be.
Then the phone rang and she said; I need to think about you and
me.
She hung up and it felt like I was choking.
Is this for real? Or was she joking?
Days past by and I couldn't sleep.
I knew for myself this love is deep.
So I called her and begged, please I want you back with me.
I said to her; my love for you is unconditionally.
For day's I didn't eat, because I couldn't take any more.
I was so weak; I fell and lay unconscious on the floor.
Seems I'm a lucky guy, because my girl came to me that night.
She walked through the door and recognized something wasn't
right!
When I woke up in a hospital I felt her head on my heart.
She notice I was awake, (crying) she said; baby without you my
world feels torn apart.

We'll Never Part

People say on your face there's a glow.
It's all because I love my baby, and I'm not afraid to let it show.
She's like the 7th heaven to me.
Her love is like a flame, which burns for eternity.
She is my air, my life.
She's my lover and soon to be my wife.
She is the lightning in a stormy night.
For her I would do all, for her I'll fight.
Her and I are soul mates forever.
That's why we're so good together.
She's like a river that roars into a sea.
I thank God that she's with me.
She found the key to my heart.
This love is ment to be, and we'll never part.
Her smile brightens up my day.
There's nothing that could make me walk away.
She's like the rain, which washes away my pain.
My heart is pounding for two, because her blood is running
though my vein.
She's everything I ever wished for.
In my life there's no room for another lover, not any more.

You Make My World Complete!

How do I know I love you?
That's simple! Cause my heart is beating for two.
My mind drifts off to space.
When I dream, I see your face.
The trust between us is very strong.
Our love is so right; I know nothing could go wrong.
All the time I spend with you.
It made me feel happy, cause you make my world colored so I'll never feel blue.
You made my world complete! That's for sure.
When I'm sick, you're my cure.
We'll take our life slowly day by day.
I always say, what comes what may.
I trust you with all my heart.
Can't wait to be there and I'll never depart.
I know it will be a different world for me.
I'll handle it, cause I love you endlessly.
No way! Will there be hard times together.
It's because our love is forever.
Baby I love you! And I will even in our next life.
I know where my heart belongs; I'll see you in heaven when I arrive.

Always Near

Always remember I'm always in your heart.
So when I'm gone please don't be torn apart.
I'll be there by your side you just have to call my name.
I'm always around you like the sun or the rain.
Without you knowing I'd be there like the wind that whisper in
your ear.
I'll never leave my love ones, cause I'm always in your heart and
near.
I'm the sun that will chase the clouds away.
When you need strength just look to the sky and pray.
I never wanted to leave yet my time is done here on earth.
I know you, but please never stop thinking of me even when you
cry out of hurt.
Instead remember the best things we shared together.
You know I'm in your heart forever and ever.
When you call my name I'll come right away.
I won't think twice I'm there to make you feel okay.
I love you please remember this.
When the rain touches your lips it would be me, who gives you a
kiss.
I'll wait in heaven till my love ones appear.
I would even wait my whole eternal life right here.
I'll watch you from the heavenly clouds, so I'll know you'll be okay.
Cause baby I love you forever and a day.

We're As One

My heart hurts for you.
I can feel all the pain you're going through.
We're bonded by one heart.
There is no way we'll ever part.
Tears are running down my cheek.
Our love grows stronger by the week.
I found you and you're perfect for me.
I want to be with you for eternity.
It's so weird yet it seems we have one soul and mind.
You're so good for me and always very kind.
My heart is pounding faster then before.
Can't live without you any more.
We're connected and we act like we're as one.
That's why we're always having so much fun.
Its like we hear each other's mind.
This is a love that is hard to find.
It's so magical and pure of love.
I want every day a bit more of you, cause I can't get enough.
We'll always be together even after this life.
I couldn't ask for more, for me you're the perfect wife.

Tell Him

Yesterday I looked upon a cloudy sky.
There I had seen a beautiful angel cry.
I asked her why are you so sad?
She replied; I miss my baby very bad.
He's still alive on earth.
I'm here in heaven and I know he's hurt.
(Crying) I didn't want to die.
It hurts me to see him cry.
Wish I could be there by his side in any kind of way.
So I can answer his prayers he says every day.
She said; wish I could send him a love letter.
So my words would make him feel so much better.
Even for just a little while.
Cause I love to see him smile.
Just to let him know I love him still very deep.
(Sad) I don't want his heart to stay broken or to weep.
I'll stand forever by his side every day and night.
I'll make sure everything stays in his life all right.
Stranger! Please I had something for you to say.
Tell him that I love him forever and a day.

All Of My Awaking Hours

I'm sitting on the beach by your side.
Watching the moon draw the tide.
The reflection of the moon is shining on the clear blue sea tonight.
I want to stay in this precious moment, so I'll hold you very tight.
A summer breeze is touching our face.
I'll always remember this time and place.
Nothing can break our love.
Counting the stars that we see in the sky above.
Your head is on my shoulder and your back is placed to my chest.
Being in this moment with you is the best.
I want to show my love in a special way.
So you know how I feel about us every day.
This night is so heavenly great.
I love you so much; you're my soul mate.
I'll never give up what we have and feel.
Our love is special and very real.
You're precious as a bouquet of flowers.
With you I'll spend all of my awaking hours.
I lay close to you holding you tight.
Waiting till the last second of our special wedding night.

Broken Wing

I found a young eagle with a broken wing.
I though to myself, aw! What a poor little thing.
There she was lying on the ground.
When I found her she barely moved around.
It seems she didn't eat for days; she really doesn't look very strong.
I was trying to figure out what went wrong.
While I was thinking I picked her up very carefully.
I took this young eagle home with me.
I had built a big cage for her where she could stay.
Until her wing is healed, so she could fly away.
For months I took care of her very good.
I made sure her wing healed, gave her food little more then I
should.
There was a bond of friendship that grew her and I together.
She completely understood that I want to make her feel better.
I had her many times on my arm watching the sunlight.
I told her; soon you're healed and big enough to take your flight.
We trained for days, yet yesterday I had to cry.
Her wing was stronger now; I had seen her glide through the sky.
She landed back on my arm and I said; now you'll have to find
your own way.
I told her, you'll stay in my heart forever, and I knew she couldn't
stay
She turned around, and she looked into my tearing eyes.
I raised my arm, and I said; go and fly to your new paradise.
She spread her wings and I seen her fly away.
I yelled to her; you'll be in my heart forever and a day.

Connected

I miss you so freaking bad she said.
Cause your name is resounding in my head.
My heart is pounding for two.
I'm so crazy about you.
Your blood is running trough my veins straight to my heart every
day.
Your face is like a picture in my mind, I look to it when I'm not
feeling okay.
Yet I'm not going to cry.
I know you're always close by.
I can feel you like you feel me.
We're connected with telepathy.
Baby it's amazing I can feel you so strong.
God knows this isn't wrong.
The feelings I feel I never felt them before.
Now I'm asking for it everyday a little bit more.
I know it's strange that we feel each other so well.
To explain to people how it feels it's hard to tell.
Baby! I love everything I feel see or hear from you.
It makes me know you're always near and that our love is so true.
That's why I'll never let you out of my sight.
I wish I was already there, and then I would hold you very tight.

Very Sick

You're lying somewhere in the intensive care.
I know it's impossible for me to be there.
I'm not able to speak with you.
My mind's going crazy and I'm feeling blue.
I live in the country of the Netherlands and that's far away.
While you're lying somewhere sick in the hospital in the country
of the USA.
There's no way of telling how bad or well you're doing today.
I'm calling your family instead of sitting here and guessing away.
I wish I could fly and be there with you.
In my heart I know this is what I want to do.
Normally we talk on the Internet cause we're not in the same
house together.
All I can do is pray and give you strength so you'll get better.
This feeling inside of me isn't very good.
It brings me to tears more then it should.
Lucky there's a friend on the Internet site.
That one is my net brother that I can call day or night.
My friend is always there for me cause he knows how I feel.
The words I write now are my feelings in real.
Soon you're home again and I'll not be alone.
I'm missing you and it hurts me to speak only on the phone.

Like A Small River

I feel blessed now I have you back.
Seems my life is on the enhance track.
You gave me purpose in my life.
And healed the cut from that rusty knife.
Girl you mean a lot to me.
That's why our love is endlessly.
I have you back and I'll never let you go.
Our love is like a small river that has a slow flow.
Just follow that river it runs like our love into a big blue sea.
There we can enjoy of our life together full of happiness and for eternity.
Free as a fish we swim, to our final place on earth.
Here we'll wait for our new rebirth.
Up in heaven we'll be together.
We're going to spend an eternity there forever.
We belong with each other this love is just destiny.
I need you in my life like you need me.
Baby my love is strong like gold.
I know you love me even when I'm bold.
I'll stay with you till death do us part.
You're the only one that's deep in my heart.

My Past Comes To My Future

When I saw you for the first time I lost my mind.
I prayed for a girl who would be like you with a special love and very kind.
I remembered the night in the bar when girl touched my hand.
I felt something weird I just couldn't place it nor could I understand.
Years have pasted by and I lived my life so wrong.
My heart wasn't with me; it was where it should belong.
I know the girl in the bar took my heart years ago.
I wonder! Does she feel the same? I need to know.
To find this girl would be hard to do, should I see her again it could only be fate.
I went on with my life and a co-worker arranged for me a blind date.
I though I found love with this girl I dated but I was wrong.
My heart was beating for some one else still very strong.
With that girl I had a blind date with; I gave her three years.
Yet all the feeling she gave me wasn't happiness, it was only sadness and tears.
Even my mother said; she's not the one for you.
God I wish my mother would stop talking in riddles, instead she should show me a clue.
In the end my mother knew all this time something wasn't right.
Cause with my x-girlfriend all we did was fight.
Then this angel came along.
She was the girl of the past I felt this strong.
I was drawing to her like it was ment to be.
My heart was beating hard and quickly.
My heart was right and she asked do you remember this?
That one night in the bar at the end of your shift, I brought you to heaven with a kiss.
At this moment we're together and whole.
Now we're joined forever with our hearts and soul.

Continuous Love

I'm writing some words so you'll know I'll never run away.
Our hearts are joined as one, forever and a day.
I love you so much, I only pray you'll understand and know.
That my love grows continuous cause my face will show.
Every day I'll let you see.
My love I have for you is for eternity.
I never knew I could feel this way.
I thank the Lord for you ever night when I pray.
I never had real love, which makes me sad.
The Lord sent me an angel in you, now I'm very glad.
I'll dream of you when I close my eyes.
I love to drift off to a newfound paradise.
You give me more love than I've ever had.
Sometime the thoughts in my head aren't so bad.
Wish I were at home with you touching your skin.
Our hearts are beating just like a twin.
You and I have a special bond with each other.
It could never been broken by another.
You and I will stay real strong.
Our hearts beat together like a song.

A Holiday Away

A new year is coming very soon you'll see.
Then it's over and done with this year for you and me.
Some people make promises for a new year.
I just wish for a better life without a tear.
I can't believe this year went so fast by.
This year I'm without my family and on the inside I cry.
It will be a lonely Christmas without my son and wife.
It's because they're the light in my life.
No Christmas dinner for me.
I'm not where I want to be.
I'm on a business trip; I'll send a present from where I am this year.
The only present for me, would be that my family was near.
I'll have to wait till my job here is done.
Then I'll go back to my wife and my little son.
Can't wait to be back home.
I'm tired of spending all my days alone.
Baby soon I'll be back for the two of you.
I understand you both miss me to.
Please have patient with me.
Remember when I'm home I'll stay for eternity.

The Vow

Baby I love you unconditionally.
I want to say you're the only one for me.
You and I have been a long time together.
I want this life with you to last forever.
Maybe the things I'm going to say you heard them before.
Yet my heart tells me to do this, so let me kneel down on the floor.
I love you from the moment you lay your eyes on me.
I was struck by a jolt of electricity.
We've been through some rough years.
You and I felt happiness' and many tears.
Even some people have tried to take us apart.
Yet I let no one break our heart.
Our interests are of the same kind.
A love like ours is hard to find.
We lost each other in the past yet we found each again.
Now it's time to understand that I'm the perfect man.
I'll die without you cause our love is so strong.
I know what I feel and I know this isn't wrong.
This love is ment to be.
That's why I want to ask; do you want to marry me?

She's My Flying Friend.

That little Squirrel you'll see that's me.
I'm here jumping from tree to tree.
I have nice soft brown fur.
Some squirrels can fly I know that for sure.
They're not like me, cause they can glide through air.
When I see them I think that's not fair.
I want to fly too! Just like those flying squirrels, so I try.
I can't do it, I wonder why?
One day I went to the flying squirrel and I asked; how did you do
that?
She showed me and pointed to her small wing that's the secret she
said.
The flying squirrel said to me, Hey don't look sad!
Just because you can't fly doesn't make you bad.
You want to play hide and seek?
Come on little squirrel count to ten but don't you peek.
So we played till the end of evening light.
I became friends with her, yet I had to call it a night.
We went back home and we both said; we'll meet again some
other day.
Thanks for the lovely day, I yelled from far away.
I'm so happy she took me in as a friend.
Couldn't wait to be back with her, I wished tonight didn't have to
end.

I Promised No Lies.

Lean your head on my shoulder.
With you I want to grow older.
Forever we'll be together just you and I.
Till the moment we both die.
I love you with all of my heart.
Even in heaven we'll never part.
Knowing our love is so strong.
Our love is written so much like a song.
You and I are ment to be.
You give me love that's unconditionally.
Together we chase away the clouds till the sky is clear blue.
Nothing can stop me from loving you.
We live our lives with ups and downs.
Every day has its laughter and frowns.
No matter what happens tomorrow.
Our love has no sorrow.
I want to speak my mind to you, because my love is so true.
I'll never tell you no lies, that's a promise I gave to you.
I know that you can see.
My love I have for you is unconditionally.

Taken By You

My girl worries every day.
That someone is trying to take my heart away.
I know its silly cause this could never happen to me.
My love for her is endlessly.
How could some one steal my heart when I have non?
My heart is in my girl's hands, and also of our son.
Doesn't she understand? I'm going to be her man till I die.
People may think they can split us up; their foolish and they may
try.
My love is for real and forever.
She and I will stay a lifetime together.
A little trust is what I ask for and all I need.
If we didn't! We'll go crazy and it would make our hearts bleed.
Guess I have to make her understand how I feel inside.
There's nothing that I wouldn't tell her; cause there's nothing for
me to hide.
With her I didn't fall once but I fell twice in love.
She seems to be my angel from above.
This has to be fate or call it destiny.
I love her and I know she loves me.
So remember my love for her is pure as gold.
The whole world may know I love our son and her till we die old.

I Cast A Spell

My girl and I walked through the park.
Slowly the night was turning completely dark.
The silver moon rose full to the sky.
I howled to the moon, I didn't understand why.
Suddenly I drop to the ground like I was in pain.
Hair started to grow everywhere; I thought I was going insane.
I felt so weird inside.
I yelled to my girl, go run and hide.
There was a lake close by.
I went to look in the water and I started to cry.
There I was turning into a werewolf, yet how could this be?
I couldn't remember right away, how could this happen to me?
Then this weird spell book came in my mind.
It was the spell I cast; I was praying that my girl knew where I left
this book behind.
Seems all of my prayers was just to late.
Soon this form is on his permanent state.
Then I saw my girl in the distance running to me.
She yelled! I found the book and the remedy.
I was so lucky, that she could break this spell.
Never again, would I want to be this close to hell.

I'm So Fortunate

No matter what you say or do.
I'll never stop loving you.
We're a million miles apart.
Your love is inscribed in my heart.
We can talk for hours on the phone or even write a letter.
What we say or write makes our love only better.
I know, its love what I feel.
My love is no illusion it's for real.
Every moment we spend together.
Holds a memory in my heart forever.
Every smile you're giving me.
Brings me to heaven so quickly.
Our love is like gold and very unique.
When you speak to me it sounds like sweet music.
Heaven showed me an angel in you.
To escape of your love I would never do.
Without you life is not meaningful.
You give your love total and unconditional.
I love you to a tee.
I'm so fortunate that you're in love with me.

Back To Life

I let no one see how I really feel.
My broken heart was completely surrounded by a wall of steel.
Then I met this sweet girl unexpectedly.
She had changed my world instantly.
I thought no one could ever find my heart.
Yet she found every little part.
She glued all the parts together.
And with a kiss she made it all better.
She brought me back to life when I was dying.
I know she loves me so much, cause I had seen her crying.
I heard her shouting; please don't take him this way.
Cause I want to spent a lifetime with him till we're old and gray.
I've seen a white light in my eyes.
Is this the way to heavens paradise?
There was this guardian angel standing on my way.
She came to me and said; I have something to say.
I have to send you back to earth.
It's to soon for you to die, that girl's prayer has been heard.
Suddenly I felt myself grasping for air.
I said to the girl who was knelling next to me, I'm going nowhere.
She asked; what you're saying to me is this true?
I said yes! God has seen the pure love for me inside of you.

We Both Know

On the Internet I chat away.
I met this girl she said; you're okay.
She wasn't looking for anything, yet she found love.
She took my heart with a feeling I never dreamed of.
We traded pictures of each other that night.
She said; I have long hair, I replied; it doesn't matter its alright.
My heart was beating fast when I saw her smile.
I couldn't speak for a long while.
I never felt love like this, didn't know it truly excised.
She was a shy girl and never been kissed.
She means everything to me, more then any other girl I had
before.
Love! Yes She gives it all to me and I don't ask for more.
She's kind and very funny.
She is so sweet like pure honey.
This is the power of love like some people would say.
This feeling is strong, I wouldn't even think about walking away.
She asked me, why do you want to understand me?
I replied to her; it's because I love you unconditionally.
Baby you had my heart and soul from the start.
You and I both know, this is love and it will never be torn apart.

It's Hard Not To Cry

It's a dark rainy day.
I wish I could chase the clouds away.
A day like this looks so sad.
Thoughts of my girl were running through my head real bad.
Every drop of rain that falls to the ground, it's my tears dripping all the way down.
I feel so sad, yet inside of me I try to find that clown.
Her name is inscribed in my heart.
A love so deep that never could be torn apart.
It comes with a feeling that no one would understand.
She's not here, yet I feel the touch of her hand.
She means everything to me.
She gives me love that feels so real and it's endlessly.
Even a Wicca spell wouldn't make me feel like this.
I was stun after our first kiss.
Her eyes are bright just like the stars, in the clear evening sky.
I miss her bad, its hard not to cry.
No one could give me this feeling, and I never felt it before.
After that kiss I wanted much more.
She's all what I prayed for in this life.
This heavenly angel I met is now my wife.

Compatible Forever

There's no reason to doubt my love.
No one can change my feelings there tight like a glove.
What I feel for you inside.
I show it all to you, there's nothing that I hide.
I also knew that you felt the same for me.
That's why our love was ment to be.
This love can never be torn apart.
I can feel the rhythm of your beating heart.
We're two people with one mind.
I found you at last, this perfect love was hard to find.
You and I are compatible forever.
We'll raise our children together.
To me life is, giving you all my love and spending my time with you.
I'll show you love, I'll never give you pain cause it hurts me to.
We don't have to say a word to each other; we don't let our minds
go astray.
We live our life like we want, we don't let it bother us what people
say.
Baby I know you can see.
My love that I have for you is for eternity.

I'm Not Like That

I'm not a person that play's with some ones heart.
This is for sure, I love my girl and we won't depart.
When I say to her; I love you I mean it to.
She's the one that makes me happy every day.
The feeling she gives me is like a musical play.
She's so sweet like a perfect flower.
It's her love that shocks me with an electric power.
Every time I look to her I drown in her sea blue eyes.
I see love in her eyes; I swear I'm telling you no lies.
Her touch is soft as silk and so heavenly.
This love, was just ment to be.
Every word she speaks to me is like poetry in my head.
She's the one that can make me smile when I'm sad instead.
Her love is like the sweetness of chocolate to me.
I love her very much and unconditionally.
There's no feeling better then her love.
It's true she is my angel from heaven above.
I'll spend a lifetime with my partner my soul mate.
We'll make it so great, cause our love is fate.

Indian Wedding

I met an Indian tribe for a reason, yet my girl didn't explain it to me.
Here I am not knowing what's going to happen, cause for me it
was a mystery.
I knew my girl had Indian blood running through her veins, she
told me yesterday.
Suddenly I understood they wanted to honor me in a special way.
Music was playing and it seems like I'm falling into a trance.
My girl was dressed in white, and in front of my eyes she started
to dance.
Food as I never tasted before, the music sounded so nice.
While I was kneeling down they honored me, I was taken by
surprise.
Feathers for me where placed on my head.
This is a wedding ritual that's what my girlfriend said.
The tribe wanted a special wedding for us tonight.
I heard wolfs howling, and there was a full moon that was shining
so bright.
The tribe yelled the lucky one is finally here.
The spirits told us he was coming! Said my girlfriend's uncle with
a cheer.
It's kind of funny; I always wanted to visit an Indian tribe in my
life.
So here I am honored, cause one of their relatives is now my wife.
Also our son has been given an Indian name.
With my new Indian name I'm proud and I carry no shame.
It was an overwhelming experience for me.
And this day I'll keep it in my heart for eternity.

Fortitude

Changes can be very great.
Sometimes it's just to late.
We can never go back in time and change a single day.
Sometimes I think when we change things it's not okay.
Life is what we make of it.
It's not always easy I must admit.
Time and patience collide together.
When we're okay life will be so much better.
Sometimes when things don't go our way.
Don't lose your patients or you thoughts for the day.
I assure you when you finally have what you're waiting for.
You'll never let it slip through you hands like sand anymore.
Its like love, don't look for it, it will find you.
Believe me it happen to many people and also to me so I know it's
true.
Give your love to your partner unconditional don't let it slip away.
A person is no ones possession but loving them is okay.
Listen to your partner with an open mind and patience and you'll
see.
Life can feel wonderful with a completion of eternity.
Love is something no one really completely understands.
A good relationship needs true strength its in your own hands.

The Fire Of Passion Ignites

I feel this heavenly desire.
It burns like an eternal fire.
My girlfriend is teasing me bad.
This is a strong feeling like I never had.
She knows exactly where to touch.
I whispered in her ear, baby I love you so much.
She drives me wild like a beast every time.
And the way she moves looks so fine.
She always stops when I'm almost there.
The ecstasy grows stronger, baby you don't play fair.
We stopped for a new position and started slowly again.
The way she makes me feel shows me that this was all part of her
plan.
She had me blindfolded, and the handcuffs made it even worse for
me.
It's so exciting! The fire of passion ignites so heavenly.
Then she took the blindfold off, I saw her sweet devilish smile.
In my ear she whispered, I'm going to make love with you for a
long long while.
It's amazing! With Oils and candles and special toys she made our
night complete.
The way she kissed and caressed my body, it was shivering yet so
sweet.
I was at a point that I couldn't handle it no more.
The climax felt like an explosion, she made me come like never
before.
She took my handcuff off while she laid her head on my heart.
She slowly stroked my chest and said; you complete my desires
from the start.
I kissed and told her: I can't live without you and I'll never walk
away.
Baby I love you, forever and a day.

The Most Horrible Moment Of Our Life

My wife and I had our first child.
Life was so great and wild.
Our child was sick and it seems very bad.
We went to the doctor and the results where sad.
The doctor said; go to the hospital your baby is very ill.
He promised to do his best with God's will.
We started to cry and we held each other tight.
It was the worst moment of our life that night.
The baby had a bad case of bronchitis and the flu.
I fell to my knees and prayed it was the best thing that I could do.
No child needs to be sick; he didn't have a chance in life it's just not fair.
My wife said; baby we can do nothing and stroked through my hair.
I knew she was in pain as much as I.
I also completely understand why.
She carried the baby for nine months with satisfaction.
In the mean time she created a bond and a connection.
Were so happy with his birth when we seen his little face.
The baby would have so much love and live in a warm place.
The chances that he was getting better where very slim.
We're in so much pain of losing him.
We couldn't blame the doctor he tried to cure our baby with all his might.
Yet we had to say farewell to our little baby boy last night.

She Satisfies Me

I was surprised when I saw the love in her eyes.
She knew I was shy so she lifted my chin and kissed me to
paradise.
I started to undress her while she caressed my chest.
Then I whispered in her ear your love is the best.
We were caressing each other's privet parts.
The rhythm was rising in our beating hearts.
Adrenalin was pumping through our veins; sweat was dripping
from our skin.
It feels like heaven, this is no sin.
It was our first time yet everything went so perfectly fine.
We were relaxing cause we drank some passionate fruit wine.
Sipping on our wine, while watching an erotic movie late in the
night.
Stroking her body while she laid her head on my chest real tight.
We made love every hour.
I whispered in her ear let make love in the shower.
The feeling was out of this world, it was so exciting every time we
came together.
She moaned while she dragged her nails down my back and
hollered I love you forever.
This night was the beginning of our passionate life.
She knows how to satisfy me as my lover and wife.
Our passion for each other is like an electric shock from heaven
above.
I'll never leave her because she rocks my world with all her love.

The Female I Dearly Love

Sitting here thinking about how my life has gone for me.
I went through ruff times and I guess that's the way it's ment to be.
Didn't like myself very well, didn't get along with many people here.
Even though they tried to be my friends I stayed clear.
My friends told me one day you'll have a reason to be happy you'll
see.
You'll find a love like a fire that will burn for eternity.
I didn't believe them; all I could see was hiding myself inside!
I guess they were right cause I've been set free just at the moment I
almost died.
A female took my heart with all her might.
It was destiny, and love at first sight.
I was so scared to let her in my heart.
I was afraid she couldn't handle me and we'd fall apart.
She's great and she showed me this love is divine.
I want to tell the whole world this woman is mine.
She's everything in a woman, I couldn't ask for more.
She helped me to open my heart like a door.
I never believed in God or angels before today.
I know now, I am here only to say.
Thank you my friends and the Father above.
For you have given me a woman with so much love.
This is like a perfect wish come true.
My girlfriend makes me feel brand new.
I love my honey with all I can.
I'm so glad that I'm her man.

We'll Be Reunited

I'm home alone every night.
This feeling that I feel, don't feel right.
I want to snuggle in my lover's arms so bad.
I pull a pillow to my chest and pretend it's her head.
It's cold outside so I ignite the fireplace.
While I watch the flames burning I can see her face.
From my eyes they're dripping some tears slowly down my cheeks.
I'm without the presence of my lover for almost a year and two
weeks.
I know what I'm missing in my life.
A bond that I lost, God! Why does it have to hurt like a cut of a
knife?
One day we'll be reunited in heaven Baby I'll meet you there.
I don't like all this waiting it's just not fair.
I'm reading love letters that you have written to me in the past.
It brings back a lot of good memories that will forever last.
When I lost her I decided to love no one else any more.
She's the only one I truly adore.
I prayed on a star, I'd see you my love, when it's my time to go.
I love you forever my angel, I just wanted you to know.

I Miss Her Terribly

It was drizzling outside today.
While I was on my way
I was thinking about my lover.
New feelings that I just had to discover.
Even at my work she was in my mind.
She's like a perfect flower that you could ever find.
There's nothing that I can do; I miss her so much.
Yet when I think of her I can feel her touch.
I can hear her sweet voice in my ear.
I whispered back, wish you where here.
She's on the other side of the word from me.
It just makes me miss her more and terribly.
I'm thinking of all the things that we could do.
Baby you know I'm so deep in love with you.
I can't wait till we're back together.
So we can spend a lifetime forever.
You know my love is unconditional.
Your love is in my heart and soul.
Don't you worry about this love of mine.
I'll make sure you always feel so fine.

She's The Only One

I have a wonderful love in my life once more.
It's been a long time since I felt this feeling before.
I met her in my life a few years ago.
It was love at first sight and I didn't want to let her go.
I wanted to stay right there and talk to this woman all night.
I knew my chances of that were very slight.
When I left her I let my heart stay behind with her that day.
I prayed to the Lord bring her back in my life and let her stay.
Well God answered my prayers; she walked back in my sight.
I swear to God! I won't let her go again as of that night.
We've been together for almost two years now.
I love her so much; I'll bend over in front her and give her a bow.
She's the love of my life and I want her to see.
She's the only one, forever for me.
Were brought back together for a couple of reasons.
Our love is strong, and we're not afraid to share it in all seasons.
Now I have found my heart back again and it will never leave me.
It's time for us to join hands and live our lives out completely.
Baby I say this to you with all my heart.
Will you marry me? And join me in a new start.

With All My Heart
(I'll Always Love You)

I made a wrong judgment in front of your eyes.
It wasn't the right thing, I now realize.
I love you with everything I feel inside of me.
I need only to control my anger very quickly.
If I could make it all go away I would.
And let us get back together the way we should.
You mean everything to me, never felt anything like this before.
I love you so much and I couldn't ask for more.
I don't want us to have arguments and scream and cuss.
I only want things to go right for the both us.
I love you with all my heart and that's no lie.
I would give up everything; for you I'd even die.
Never felt anything like this before in my life.
One day I can only hope you want to be my wife.
I really don't want to ruin what we have together.
Cause I love you so much and I want you in my life forever.
I never will forget that very first hug we shared.
When I think about it, it brings tears to my eyes and I feel how much I cared.
You're in my heart and in my soul.
Without you my world is not whole.

My Lovely Day Out

I was walking down the streets of London today.
The sun had chased the clouds away.
You can hear the big Ben clocks ringing.
The sun is shining and I'm whistling and singing.
Cause the lovely day was so warm and fine.
I was going to sit outside a bar to drink some wine.
There I was waiting for my precious flower.
She said I'd meet you there in an hour.
We had planed for a movie and a dinner tonight.
While I was listening to the café music she walked in my sight.
I love the way she was dressed today.
She knows how to take my heart away.
Her eyes are shining like stars in a clear sky.
She's the only one for me, for her I would die.
We went for a walk in the park on this lovely day.
She whispered in my ear, I love you in every way.
I knew her for a long time and she makes my life complete.
It was love at first sight; the first time we met was so neat.
I could never trade her not even for the worlds gold.
I want to spend my lifetime with her till I'm gray and old.

From The Bottom Of My Heart

I'm so in love with you.
You make my whole life start to come true.
You're the inspiration in my heart.
You know when to stop my anger when it begins to start.
You're everything I ever could have wished for.
God gave you to me to adore.
You're the woman I always dreamed of.
Seems you're been sent to me from heaven above.
Don't ever change; cause I love you like you are.
You're my best friend and my lover and my shinning star.
These are a few things I wanted to say what you are to me.
You make me so happy and you let me live free.
You have so much love for me; it puts me on a high cloud.
The whole world may know that I love you; so I'll yell it out very
loud.
I mean this from the bottom of my heart.
Please never leave me; never depart.
You're made for me.
You're my destiny.
I don't want to let you go cause I have so much love for you.
Let me be your man for the rest of your life, and beyond this life
too.

Unconditionally

There's a fire that burns in my heart and soul.
It's a heavenly desire that has no control.
My girlfriend knows me to the tee.
A feeling of love better then she gives me could never be.
She knows how to make me smile when I'm down.
Only she can stop me from crying or having a frown.
The way she pleases me is the way I love.
I love her and I can't say this enough.
She's more then just being my wife.
I can say she's my soul mate for life.
She's the one and I want her to know.
I love her so much, and I'll never let her go.
There's nothing that can change my mind or heart.
She's everything to me, and this love will never be torn apart.
My love for her is unconditional, and I'm not afraid to say.
I never knew what love really ment until today.
She's all that I need and I don't ask for more.
She sounds so fine like seas that roar.
I'm happy the way we're connected together.
This is true love that will last forever.

My Bleeding Heart

A bleeding heart is what I have without you.
You make all my dreams and wishes come true.
I love you so much yet you're half a world away.
There's this emptiness cause I want to be there and stay.
I miss you and I can feel it in my bleeding heart.
Never in my life will I let this love fall apart.
People say were destined to be together.
A love so strong that will last forever.
My heart will drip blood until I come home where I feel free.
Then our hearts will join as one for eternity.
I can say I LOVE YOU a 100 times a day.
Please tell me the same; never change or our love will slip way.
We can feel this special touch.
It means the world to me, now you know why I love you so much.
You're the wind beneath my wings.
It's as precious as a bird when it sings.
My heart will stop bleeding for you.
When I'm there forever, and this is true.
I'm waiting until I'll be there by your side; and all will be okay.
I'll never stop telling you, that I love you forever and a day.

What America Means Too Me

I'm from the Netherlands and I like to travel to the USA.
Even though I'm speaking Dutch my English is getting better by
the day.
I love America for it's beautiful seasons.
Even the people are outspoken and nice, and that gives me good
enough reasons.
In the USA Christmas, is very meaningful and that's so great.
I met an American girlfriend by God's heavenly fate.
Of all the people in the USA I love her the most; her and I will
marry one day.
You have to live by the laws and order but I think that's okay.
I've been in a country music spell right from the start.
I really can say, USA you won my soul and heart.
New York they call it the big apple; and who's that lady on your
shore.
She's the statue of liberty a beautiful lady that the Americans adore.
Her torch brightens up the sky and my name is inscribed in her
book.
I've seen something on a pole so I took a second look.
The American flag waved with its stars and stripes very proud.
This overwhelming feeling brings me on a high cloud.
Chicago is the home of my favorite female TV host.
And the rest of the famous people who I love and adore the most
Las Vegas is where it's warm because it's lying in the wasteland.
But where do they get the power and water? That's hard to
understand.
What does the USA mean to me? Is it the music the movies the
people or is it the art.
There's too much to say why I really love America with all my heart.
There's this thing about Freedom that just speaks to my heart.
If freedom could spread all over the world, it would be a nice start.

I Survived

Oh poor little scary me.
I'm a helpless Caterpillar in a tree.
Danger is around me every day.
I must eat a lot so I can fly away.
When I eat enough I spin a cocoon.
I'm dreaming to be a beautiful butterfly very soon.
A new day is beginning; suddenly a hand picked me up from the ground.
I was afraid what would happen to me, so I started to roll around.
Then I was placed in a glass cage, and I though to my self, why!
I heard a voice telling me; here's a save spot till you can fly.
It's amazing this person fed me real good.
I spun my cocoon on a piece of wood.
Finally my cocoon was all ready and I slept for days.
The person looked to see if I was okay; while popping out my cocoon I saw her face.
I felt my body changing into this beautifully butterfly.
Its time for me to come out of my cocoon, I had to do it alone or I would die.
The struggle was hard yet I made it on my own.
I know this was the right thing cause the lady left me alone.
Then she took me out of the cage and let me dry my wings from the warmth of the sun.
My wings were strong enough, I flew to the lady's hand, thanked her for everything she done.
Because the lady helped me to survive I can fly now through the sky.
I'm so happy to see the whole world from here so I'm blessed that I didn't die.

Deep In My Heart

The sun is shining bright in the snow today.
My son asked; massy will you go out with me and play.
He took his coat and his cloves and hollered to me.
Massy Massy it's snowing so pretty please come and see.
I love the smile on his face, and the twinkle in his eyes.
He loves me as a real dad now I realize.
We're building a snowman, and taking a ride in a sledge.
Making snow angels, I'm feeling like a kid right away.
We laugh and giggle cause we have so much fun.
I know deep in my heart he's not my child, yet I see him as my
own son.
It really doesn't bother me.
Cause I do love him endlessly.
I know his love to me is no game.
You can hear it in his voice when he calls my name.
He despises his real father and I completely understand why.
He doesn't need a dad that's abusive and make him cry.
I'll be the best daddy he can dream of.
Cause like his mother I'm touched by his love.
Nothing will stand in front of me.
I'll protect my love ones for eternity.

What Loves Exactly All About?

Love is a feeling that's hard to understand.
You could have some sweat in the palm of your hand.
A strange feeling in your stomach like butterfly's moving around.
When you want to talk to your lover your voice could have a
shaking sound.
It could happen that you feel yourself flying.
And when you're not with your lover you could be crying.
Every second is to long to wait that's for sure.
When your lover is sick you want to be their only cure.
Time goes always much to fast.
Yet true love will forever last.
Your heart and mind has been inscribed with one name.
A deep love makes your partner feel the same.
Your mind is with your lover: Your heart will beats for two.
Eating or drinking is something what you hardly do.
No time for friends or going out.
I asked myself what's love exactly all about.
Well I love the feeling I've felt from my lover.
Yet bad feelings belong in the same package I discover.
Hold on to the feelings when you find true love.
And when you need help pray to the Lord above.

I Won't Let You Go

Baby will you please try to understand.
I never want you to slip like sand through my hand.
I'm falling down on my knees while I'm crying on this coldish
floor.
You're the one and only for me, and I won't ask for more.
Yet you want to walk out of my life.
Stop twisting with that rusty old knife.
My emotions are hardly under control.
Now I'm walking around for days with a hole in my soul.
I'm going to give you a final chance to try.
Cause without you I know I'd die.
There's no person better then you.
I just wish you could see this too.
You're my angel; you're my only cure.
I need you back in my life, and that's for sure.
Can't live a day without your touch.
You're the love of my life, and I love you so much.
I'd be lost if you weren't here with me I must confess.
There would be sadness, and no happiness.
Please try it one more time when you can.
Cause all I want to be is your lover and your man.

Deep Within My Soul

When I look in your eyes, I suddenly realize, the way you love me.
I can feel it from your soul; it's so wonderful, that your love is so
deep like the sea.
We'll be together, a lifetime forever, that's for sure.
You healed the pain, which was in my main vein, cause you're my
cure.
I could spend hours, in a field of flowers, every day.
No one can take my heart, or ever tear it apart, cause I don't listen
to what people say.
The way you make me feel, it's so magical and real, and I tell it to
every one.
When we're all together I'll cry, cause you complete my life that
why, together with your son.
Never doubt my reasons of love, it's tighter then a glove, that fits
very well.
I'll cross every fire, to win your hearts desire, even through the
deepest part of hell.
Nothing can stop me, not even the tallest tree, not now or never.
I'll say to you, my love is always true, from now and forever.
Baby you're the one, remember this is not for fun, but I say it
from deep within heart.
Don't listen to what people say, you and I are okay, this love was
ment to be from the start.
Darling you're the apple of my eye, it really is no lie, cause you're
the one I need.
When I lose you out of my sight, I would cry every night, without
you my heart would bleed.
You know what I'm going to say, I love you every day, and I'll say
it as much as I can.
And when you still don't understand, I will ask you for your hand,
cause I want to be your man.

Love Is The Key

I feel this particular way, when you say in Dutch I love you to me.
(Ik hou van jou) those words make me shiver so heavenly.
I truly never say it enough, those four words, I mean it from my
heart to you.
There's no second person that makes me feel the way you do.
It feels like an electrical power surge very deep inside.
It's even better then an adrenalin rush of the fastest roller coaster
ride.
Even better then the biggest waves of a roaring sea.
You complete my life with love that's so unconditionally.
No mountain peaks above the love we have with our height.
No road is longer then the love you show me every day and night.
You say to me I LOVE YOU its much better then a beautiful love
song.
With love I see things going right, and will never go wrong.
No stars in the sky can match your love I carry inside.
We gave our love to each other; we have nothing to hide.
We feel the same connection in our souls and heart.
By God's fate we found love; and nothing can tear us apart.
My darling I'll tell you every day that you're the one for me.
My love is burning as a flame; I couldn't wish for more you set me
free.
I'll never let you slip through my hands; you're the one I adore.
We're two people that have a love so strong, I've never felt that
before.
All I want is to speak my mind to you, because my love is so true.
I'll never tell you any lies, that's a promise I'll give to you.

The Truthful Story (A destiny's Love)

Ever heard of fairytales that came true?
Well let me tell an amazing story about a Dutch guy to you.
Few years ago he worked as a Stewart on a ship.
Work was great and hard in the meantime he enjoyed the trip.
One day this beautiful American woman came in his sight.
He never forgot the memories with her on that special night.
Then he lost her out of his sight but not out of his heart.
He was in love yet he felt bad when she needed to depart.
If only he gave his address so she could find him back.
Yet instead he started to live on a wrong track.
Years went by and he was thinking of her with his whole heart.
Knowing this feeling inside of him could never be torn apart.
He told me that he couldn't look for her cause he had no lead.
He still felt her in his soul, and his heart started to bleed.
The memories were inscribed deeply inside of this man.
You know love by heart when it's ment to be, yes you can.
On a chat program this man found some friends and chatted away.
A very nice guy introduced him to this lady one day.
Because of that he has seen his lost lover's face and heard her voice.
He was dating at the time a girl, so he had to make a choice.
The decision he made completely changed his life.
He asked this woman; will you marry me and be my wife.
This woman and her child are living with him happily together.
See a fairytale can come true! And they live all together with a love
that last forever.

Lullaby

Try to sleep little one just for tonight.
Everything will be all right.
Don't be sad my little one.
Tomorrow you'll wake up by the sun.
It's a beginning of a brand new day.
I love you little one I mean what I say.
And when you start to weep.
I'll rock you in my arms until you're falling to sleep.
Dream about the stars in the sky.
While I sing for you a lovely little lullaby.
Try to sleep sweet child of mine.
I'll be here when you're not fine.
Close your little baby eyes.
Let yourself drift to paradise.
I'll stay with you for just a little while.
Cause I love it when you sleep and you smile.
Even I'm going soon to bed for tonight.
Together we'll wake up by the morning light.
I'll tell you with my whole heart I love you for evermore.
You're my sweet little baby that I truly adore.

A Night Full Of Passion

My adrenaline is pumping with a rush for you.
Seems you know exactly what to do.
You touch me with your hands, a kiss from your sweet lips.
I'll stroke your golden blond hair with my fingertips.
You know the spots that turns me on, cause you know where to find.
Everything I thinking of you do it cause you can read my mind.
Making love slowly it's so fantastic that it brings us closer together.
Wish we could stay in this exciting moment forever.
Every little feeling makes it hard for me to handle my sexual
control.
I love you with my whole body and soul.
Electricity goes though my body like never before.
My heart is beating faster and harder and I want your touch even
more.
You drive me wild cause you let the beast of desire grow inside of
me.
I want to move faster, I can't handle it, yet you're still moving very
slowly.
With your nails in my chest you bring the beast outside of me.
This feeling is better then any ecstasy.
Damn baby I love you; your love is like an eternal flame.
Everything about you is perfect even your sweet name.
After a long night full of firing passion we like to kiss.
Before we sleep you lay your head on my chest, cause you know I
love this.

I Don't Want You Back

My question is, what went wrong here.
Is there a reason why I should be in fear?
Yet you're leaving today out the door.
Saying: I don't love you no more.
I have this pain inside of losing you.
I feel lost; God what must I do.
I'll curse you! Cause you hurt me so bad.
I thought this was a strong love that we had.
Yet you needed to cheat behind my back.
Where did our love start to fall of the track?
Well then leave me for good! For you're not fair.
Cause for your reasons! I have no mood and I don't care.
Don't even think that you could come back as a friend.
This is it; you messed it up to much now, it's truly our end.
You told me, what you done to me.
I still don't understand how this could be.
It doesn't matter that I'm alone now.
You've broken our promises and our vow.
I told myself I'll never fall in love again.
Because of all this trouble, I don't need another woman or man.

Pain To My Heart

This is the hardest part in any ones life.
It even hurts like a cut of a knife.
This love wasn't ment to be.
You and I are so different can't you see.
I can't take this any more.
You don't treat me like you did before.
All you've done is give pain to my heart.
I think its better when we're apart.
I don't want to see you anymore, not even as a friend.
Please leave my life because our love has come to an end.
I can't live with a person when the love is gone.
When I'd stay we only fight and that's so wrong.
I feel our love is gone, and that's no surprise.
I know I hurt you, I can see it in your eyes.
You asked me a lot of questions while you were crying.
Things like; what's the reason we broke up tell me without lying.
I can't answer! Cause it's of me and not of you.
There's nothing more that I can say or do.
I wish you all the luck from heaven above.
May God guide you; so you'll find a better love.

In A Blink Of A Eye

I know I hurt you yesterday.
I don't want to push you away.
Let me hold you close to me.
Cause I do love you endlessly.
My love for you is so freaking strong.
Yet my words to you from yesterday were so wrong.
Baby! You know I don't like it when we fight.
That's why I tossed and turned in my sleep last night.
I had never ment to push you or give you a shove.
Please come back to me cause you're my only love.
I know why we fight its because my mood changes in a blink of a
eye.
It could occur, that I'm very happy and suddenly I might start to
cry.
I know from deep within my heart and soul that we both had a
bad life.
Losing you would be worse than a cut of a rusty old knife.
Every relationship has its ups and downs.
But like other people we have our laughers and frowns.
I'll do everything to let you see.
There's no perfected love better then yours to me.
Baby will you please believe me when I say.
I'll love you forever and a day.

Sorry Isn't Hard To Say

I looked in her deep blue eyes last night.
We had a fight but now everything's all right.
Sometimes it's hard to say what we feel inside.
Most of the time that we fight it's because our words don't collide.
She was throwing a fit about what I said.
Seems to me she turned the words in her head.
I know that I'm saying things in the wrong way.
And to say sorry isn't hard to say.
I try to calm her till she can listen to me.
Doesn't she understand I didn't want to hurt her intensely?
I told her, baby we could work this out tonight.
Let's talk about it, without screaming all right.
She knows we had problems like this before.
We've agreed not to walk away any more.
I'll let her see that everything will be okay.
So let me explain what I'm attempting to say.
I just miss you when we're not together.
Baby you know I love you forever.
So let's solve this before we go to sleep.
Cause this isn't a feeling that we need to keep.

Don't You See?

I'll show you unconditional love.
Cause for me you're an angel from heaven above.
Sometimes it's hard to find the words to say.
Just remember I'll love you forever and a day.
I'll climb the highest mountain, cross the biggest sea.
Baby let me show you a love for eternity.
You don't have to guess, you just have to ask.
Don't be afraid it's not such a hard task.
I want your love every night.
Let me embrace you whether you feel bad or right.
Maybe you don't know what you mean to me.
I know I'll love you endlessly.
I'm 100% in love with you.
I hope you can feel it; cause I send it every day brand new.
Never had a feeling like this before.
Since I felt your love I don't ask for more.
And when you still don't believe in me.
I suppose I have to make a remedy.
Cause I promised myself that I would never walk away.
My heart told my mind that I'm in love and this feeling is okay.
I'll never find a better love then yours, girl I ment what I told you
tonight.
Cause my heart and mind agreed; our love was ment to be at first
sight.

Don't Give Up On Me

No matter which problems we're going through.
Just keep in mind I'll always love you.
There will always be bumps in the road where we're walking.
The best way to make our love perfect is to keep on talking.
It's better to speak your heart to me.
Then live with guilt or misery.
I love you with every beat of my heart.
We have this endless love given to us by God hands right from the
start.
I'll never let you go no matter how hard I have to fight.
We love each other so much; let's turn these bad feelings back to
right.
Your name resounds in the middle of my mind.
Without you I can't live I would die or feel left behind.
No one could come closer to my heart cause they don't have the key.
You're the lucky one girl cause your key opens my heart for eternity.
I hope that you understand me by now.
That nothing can break our promises and our vow.
At this moment being without you would be hard for me.
That's why I miss you so bad baby can't you see.
I want to ask you today an Important question in our life.
Will you marry me so you'll be my lover and my wife?

Searching For You All My Life

When I set and gaze to the sky.
I see the twinkle that comes from your eye.
You told me I never have to run or hide.
You make me feel like a king inside.
Your love for me is pure and forever.
You and I will always be in love together.
My search for a good woman has come to an end.
I found her right here as a good lover and friend.
She said to me; and I quote to you.
Doesn't matter what you look like, as long as your heart is true.
I was searching for you all my life with my heart and soul.
I did everything in my control.
When I found you back it was a blast.
Cause I knew you from my past.
The whole world must know I found you back by now.
So I'll ask for your hand in a special vow.
Never again will I let you go.
Cause I want you to know.
I love you with my body and soul.
My heart is beating for you way out of control.
This feeling is better then any dream I ever dreamed of.
You must be sent from heaven above.

God Can You Hear My Prayer!

I pray Lord because I can't take the distance any more.
I'm crying here, I'm down on my knees on a cold stone floor.
Lord I pray for a miracle, a sign for my girl and I.
I want to be with my family; cause inside without them I die.
We met each other already several times in real.
Every time I see her I knew it was love that I could feel.
Don't let me sit here alone in the darkness.
A lifetime without my lover I can't do I must confess.
With a prayer I ask for a way.
A miracle so I can stay in the USA.
I'd give everything just to get there.
Lord I want to be with my family, how! I don't care.
I begged my darling not to give up on me.
I love her so much and unconditionally.
Never wish for something more specially as now.
She knows I love her that's why we took a cyber vow.
It wasn't only for my sweetheart, also for her little boy.
You know Lord; I'd never break any heart like a toy.
God can you hear my prayer! Please send me some help today.
An angel, a sign! Show me the way so I'll be with my family in the
USA.

If You're Not The One

If you're not the one! That I adore.
Why does my heart pound faster then before?
I believe our love was ment to be.
You helped to make a better man out of me.
Never had dreams that came true.
Now I know I LOVE YOU.
My heart floats like an open sea.
With all the love you give to me.
Lets sail around the world together.
You and I were ment to be forever.
Just a touch of your hand, the sweet smile on your face.
It makes me feel happy with a feeling I won't erase.
I thank God for you; I feel totally blessed.
Deep In my heart I know that our love will forever last.

You're Not Here

Baby I miss you so bad.
When I think about you I feel real sad.
I want to keep you close in my sight.
But I know you have to work all night.
Sometimes when you're not here.
All I want to do is shred a tear.
My heart beats so fast and hard every day.
It's going to break when you're far away.
I'll try to settle my self and think clear.
Maybe I'll even drink a beer.
I'd rather wait for you to come home.
So you and I can be alone.
I want you to know how I feel.
Cause my love for you is real.
My heart beats with a different sound.
When you're not around.
When I miss you my face shows a frown.
That's why I'm hoping you're back soon from town.

God Sent You An Angel

The first time you looked in my eyes.
I knew heaven sent me a surprise.
I'll do everything to keep this love alive.
So I'll ask you: will you marry me and be my wife.
Sometime I think you can't see.
That's you're so beautiful to me.
Forever I'll be your love.
God has sent an angle from above.
He knows what he did, and what's going to happen tomorrow.
He sent me to you, so your life has no more sorrow.
By God's helping hand we're on our way.
He said to me; you must stay.
Be her guardian angel for eternity.
One day you two will become a family.
Here I am I'll never go away.
I'll give her, heavenly love every day.
I gave up my immortal life.
So I could die together with my wife.

I Don't Want To Miss A Thing

I'll stay awake just to hear you breathing.
I can't stop this lovely feeling.
I Watch your body while you're sleeping.
Laying my hand on your chest so I can feel you heart beating.
I'll spend my life in this sweet surrender.
I know you still feel the same from 14th November.
I can stay lost in this moment forever.
Because I know we belong together.
Every moment I spend with you, is a moment I treasure.
Everything I do for you I'll do it with pleasure.
I wonder what you are dreaming.
It is me that you are seeing.
Then I kiss your lips and thank God, we're together.
I want to spend a lifetime with you forever.

God Send Me An Angel From Heaven Above

She thanked God for that angel he sent from above.
That angel is a man and he showed her real love.
God may she keep that angel for life?
If she could she would ask him to be his wife.
Why God? Why did you send him to this earth?
It's his love that makes poetry out of his words.
Never take that angel away from her life.
Cause if you do, you will cut her heart in half with a knife.
She would always pray.
That her angel would stay.
Send him to her; he can fix her broken heart in time.
She need him forever like the sunshine.

A Lover's Prayer

When you need me in the day.
Then just sit down and pray.
When you need me in the night.
Just close your eyes I'll be there in your sight.
When you come here, I'll know you're going to stay.
That's been my only prayer; and I say it every day.
Baby I love you with all my heart.
You're always in my prayers right from the start.
When your heart hurts for me and I know it does.
Just raise your hands to heaven above and pray for both of us.
When the time is right I'll fly.
I'll go right through the heavens blue sky.
When you're crying, lean on me.
I can feel your feelings instantly.
You know I pray to God every day.
A lover's prayer is all I needed to say.

You Took My Heart Away

I came here trying to think clear.
What I have is an angel so very near.
I had a bad life.
My heart was hurting like it's being cut with a knife.
Then there appeared you.
And my heart stuck to you like glue.
From the moment I met you I could tell.
I already knew you very well.
You were the one for me.
You took my heart can't you see.
My love for you is so deep in my heart.
That's why I know God won't keep us apart.
When you're not there on the Internet or by the phone.
I always pray for you to come home.
You and I will never be far apart.
I can feel your love in my heart.
I love you baby this is true till I die.
And when our kids leave the house its just you and I.

Music

There're songs in my mind.
Not just one but several different kinds.
Even on the radio I hear our favorite song.
All day and night long.
The songs are reminding me of you.
It reminds me that my love for you is so true.
The radio plays rock music, soul and pop.
Deep inside my heart I know my love will never stop.
I hear the words and poems coming while I'm lying in bed.
My mood starts change from sad to glad in my head.
I listen to the words I heard today.
I remember the song titled (I'm walking away).
Also I heard the songs from 14th November.
A day I'll always remember.

The Feeling

I'm feeling in the wrong mood.
And it's not one that's good.
You hate to see me like that.
I know my mood is very bad.
It was my fault and I'm not proud of it.
But I felt pushed and shove with a bad spirit.
What I have said has been said.
But why is it still in my head.
I never wanted to hurt you like that.
I know I did and now I'm sad.
The feelings I feel are hard to say.
Please remember though; I'll never walk away.
I'm sorry for last night.
Lets make it up and forget the fight.
You know I love you girl.
Cause you're so precious as a perfect pearl.
I'll be more open to you; I'll promise you this.
So come here honey, lets make it up with a kiss.

No One Come Close Like You

You make my life so meaningful.
You have my heart body and soul.
I never had these feelings before.
Each day I want you even more.
Your name is resounding in my head.
And it will! Every day until I'm dead.
Never doubt that I won't marry you.
Without hesitation I say; yes I do.
It's two hearts that I won.
It's the love from you and your little son.

The Best Friend I Ever Had

I know this guy and once I was very mad.
But he is my best's friend I ever had.
For one year we lost touch with each other.
Then suddenly he was standing in front of me; I yelled hey brother.
He said, just checking to see if you still alive and to see your face.
Thank God! I remember where you lived; it's the same place.
This friendship is worth a lot to me.
Now he's back and all is the way it should be.
Like bashing brothers we're back together like before.
Our friendship will grow stronger each day even more.
We know the pain in each other's lives; but we always reminisce
the good old days.
Lets go for a ride on our bikes and let the wind blow softly in our
face.
Making fun like we always do.
When I move to USA, I'll always be in touch with you.
Even though when I'm going to live so far away.
My best friend in my heart you always stay.
Don't be surprised when you hear a knock at your door.
Your best friend could be back with his family; that you will adore.

My Passion Desire For You

I think of you ever night and day.
There're some words only for you to hear me say.
I need you so come sit near.
I want you baby right here.
My desire is to make love to you.
You all ways make me feel brand new.
I love the touch you give to me.
It sends me shivers to ecstasy.
Your touch makes me know what I have missed.
For the first time I felt the love when we kissed.
When you're at your highest peak.
Don't let go of this its something to keep.
Until our bodies comes closer together.
I'll say to you sweetheart I love you forever.

A Woman's Heart Taken By An Angel

I'm sitting here looking at you with a plan.
God gave me the greatest man.
I could not believe that God gave you to me.
I need your touch and love for eternity.
I just want to tell you in a way.
That I want you here so please stay.
You never heard me say this before.
That I'll love you each day just a little bit more.
You're so wonderful to me.
God give you wings can't you see.
I couldn't ask for a better person here on earth.
Because I knew you would never flirt.
I hope you'll always love me for who I am.
You mean everything to me; I know that people never would
understand.
I love you for whom you are.
Soon you'll be close but now you're far.
I couldn't bear to be without you.
I love you baby; can't say it enough cause I really do.
No one will understand the love that we share.
Some time I wish they could feel half of our love and not despair.
You as a man taking on a child for you own.
I know you never leave him alone.
God you're so wonderful and kind.
You're the best man a woman ever could find.
And my son loves you like you're his real daddy.
That's a great thing! Cause you love him already.
When I lay down you're in my dreams.
You just don't know how much that means.
God sent you to me.
Now I love you for eternally.

Our Love Is So Unique

Let me be you're lover and your man.
And do that night all over when we can.
I just want to embrace you tight.
Do you know you look so beautiful at night?
I miss you so bad and I wish you where here.
Cause you're the only one my precious dear.
I want to tell you how much I love you today.
Listen to my words what I'm about to say.
Please stay in my life forever.
Our love is the best I can't find any better.
I want to be forever by your side with all my might.
To show you my love, every night till morning's daylight.
Our love is so unique.
It's in ever kind of music.
Some people say our love is like a fairytale.
I love your words on the mic and through the mail.
I want and need to hold you very soon.
By the light of a bright clear moon.
I'll never let you go.
Because Baby, I love you so.

Because Our Love Is So New

I'll take my baby to the ocean.
We're going to lie there and watch the motion.
While we hold each other tight.
And kiss through out the night.
We watch the rising of the moon.
It comes up in the sky real soon.
We're lying on our backs, and we see a falling star.
We'll wish upon it from a far.
We both know our wishes will come true.
Because our love is so brand new.
Our feelings and thoughts are so common to each other.
Knowing that we couldn't love another lover.
We'll give it to no one else we both swear.
So for us a lifetime together is what we share.
We'll marry and go nowhere and you know why.
We're a perfect pair till the day we'll both die.

Wish I Were There Right Now

I love you more then you'll know.
As I always will and I'm not afraid to show.
Sometime I have no words so say.
How I feel inside every day.
I have so many feelings inside.
It feels like a roller coaster ride.
There're no words to explain how I feel.
Deep inside my heart I know my love is real.
Million words couldn't say.
How I'm feeling today.
That's why I'll show you my love in this poem.
Remember when you're not here I feel alone.
Let me stroke your hair and softly kiss you lips.
Touching your skin with my fingertips.
That is how much I love you girl.
For me you're like a prefect pearl.
I'll hold you tight every night.
Never again will I let you out of my sight.
I know your spirit is here with me.
Baby I'm in love with you can't you see.
I'll never run or hide.
I'll be soon by your side.
Let me make your life complete.
Because I know our love is so neat.
I'll never leave you, no way!
I'm coming soon and I'll stay.
I'll let no one stop me! And no one will come between you & me.
My heart tells me what to do; our love is unconditionally.
I'll do the things that we need to do so we'll be together.
When I lie in your arms I'll stay forever.

Missing You Very Bad

Wish you where here in my sight.
Through the day and the night.
I was shopping with my best friend today.
I still missed you in every way.
It's your voice and your smile.
I don't like it when you're gone even for a while.
I know I'm in love with a woman who feels the same.
My heart beats faster when I think of her name.
Can't wait to be home once more.
You're the one that I adore.
I love you so much I know you'll understand.
You're my lady, and I'm man.

Very Cold Nights

The nights are very cold.
I need you here to hold.
Yet you're not here with me tonight.
Wish you where here then I'd be all right.
So that's why I pull my pillow close to my chest.
Wishing your head was here to rest.
Miss your warm body close against mine.
Soon we're all going to feel fine.
Baby I want to hold you tight.
I hate the lonely cold bitter night.
I want to snuggle close to you.
That is what I want to do.
When I lie close to you; it makes my life so complete.
Then I won't worry, because I hear your heart beat.

A Fairytale Of Love Came True With You And Me

I want to surprise you with a visit at your door.
Baby I know you'll drop to your knees to the floor.
Your love for me is so sweet.
I know this and I think its neat.
I've dreamed for a long while for a woman like you.
I even would walk through hell to show you my love is true.
Only a fairytale could explain this love of mine.
It will all happen within time.
It comes from our sweet love and the tenderness of our touch.
It makes our hearts beat so fast and we love it so much.
So Romeo and Juliet move on over.
My baby fulfills me, so I gave her my lucky clover.
When a fairytale appears in reality.
Grab a hold of it, and you'll be happy watch and see.
Dreaming of the time that may come true.
In the fairytale I'm in love with you.
In that tale I found a portal that leads to your door.
And there you where waiting for me, the one you adore.

Time You Came Home

To a friend we knew a long time ago.
We really never let you go.
Long time not seen but back today.
Hope this new friendship is forever and you'll stay.
Real friends will come back.
When their life is on the right track.
Their past will be gone astray.
Real friend are forever and they'll stay.
Welcome back in our life again.
I say this from my heart my friend.
So let it be like old times and have the fun and joy.
We really missed your presents and your singing boy.
We had a friend that told us to be still.
Because you would come back it was your will.
I'll say this to you our dearest friend.
We'll be here till the end.

Sacrifice

Sometime we need to sacrifice.
The choices we decide aren't always nice.
It's hard to choose.
What do we win! What do we lose?
Sometimes you feel bad in a way.
When people say what they say.
Don't let them lead you away from me.
It's not nice to use a mind play can't you see.
It's not that you betrayed and left them behind.
Are you sure what you want; and did you make up your own mind?
I don't want to hurt you or take you from your friends.
Yet I can't help it my love is so intense.
What is life without you?
We all need friend's that's true.
I'll sacrifice my friendship to be with you every day.
You know I'll never walk away.
I'll choose you above everything sweetheart.
There's nothing or no one that can tear our love apart.

A Night Without You

I was talking to you on the Internet.
I lost my power I bet.
Oh God there's a storm and its real bad.
Now I can't talk to you and that makes me sad.
I need you to hold me tight.
Take away my all my fears for tonight.
I can't bear it when I can't talk to you my love.
You're the only one that I adore; you're my angel from above.
I need you baby forever and a day.
I said to you; could you call me tonight just say okay.
You couldn't answer cause the cable when down.
I was getting angry about my cable so I had a big frown.
I'll wait till you call; and I'm hoping you do.
That lets me know you miss me to.
When you're not here with me.
My heart beats so hopelessly.
My pain inside is so hard and I cried.
My mind feels like it has just died.
I want you by my side to comfort me.
Baby I love and need you for eternity.

A Dark Night By Myself

I'm sitting here all on my own.
Wishing you where here so I don't feel alone.
I need you baby! I'm in fear.
All I do is shred a tear.
I hate these feelings when you're not around.
All I do is cry and frown.
I pray to the Father up in the sky.
Bring back my baby tonight before I die.
Separation isn't a good thing.
I like it better when I can hear my baby sing.
She makes me smile.
Even for a little while.
So as you all can see.
I need my baby here with me.

I Don't Want To Run Away

I had a rough past.
All I want to do is run real fast.
Just to get away from the hurt and the pain.
If I don't, my brain will go insane.
I'm not saying you're the blame.
My love was never a game.
I know it's me and I have to think.
Sometimes I don't even blink.
All I look for is the easy way out.
Then I scream and I shout.
I heard her say to me: please have no mistrust.
My heart is filled with love, it feels like it's going to bust.
Baby sometimes I feel so blue.
I can't help it and this is true.
I'm not the man I used to be.
Will you help me? And set me free.
Hold me tight! Don't let me go.
I need you bad baby you just don't know.
You're the air that I breathe in my life.
I want you to marry me and become my wife.

Wake Up Babe

I'm in my room listen to songs.
All I want to do is sing all day long.
I see my baby she's asleep again.
Seems like that's a never end.
But my songs go to my head.
Then I get up to dance all over to the bed.
I crawled up to my baby nice and slow.
Kissing her slowly to wake her up because I need her so.
She opens her eyes with a smile.
I want to lay close for a while.
She says; come here baby and kiss my lips.
Stroke me with your fingertips.
Watching my baby slowly moving her body all around.
We're going to make love all up and down, God I love that sound.
She is so gentle and always thinks of me.
She brings me up first to ecstasy.
We're happy and not afraid to say.
Lovemaking for us is here to stay.

I Have No Regrets

When I look in the sky above.
What I see is your face in the clouds; I'm in love.
I get down on my knees and bow to my girl.
You're my love my precious pearl.
You helped to set my soul free.
Baby please! Stay with me.
I need you in every way you can think of.
You are my love and I can't say it enough.
I have no regrets or a second thought about you.
Only love till my death yet you already knew.
No more feelings of sadness or pain.
For you and our son forever love will remain.

Spellbound

Every time I fall in love it gets tough.
I make life for my baby very rough.
A spell has been cast.
I hope you break it fast.
The spell hurts my baby that I adore.
I think it must stop forever more.
There's so much pain in my life.
I wonder how can I survive all the strife.
It is time to say goodbye.
Cause all I do is make you cry.
I want to stop this spell of hurting my love one.
I wish I knew how I could do this because it's no fun.
What if we never have met in life?
I could never ask you to be my wife.
Would it be so different as it is now today?
Can't bare to leave I want to stay.
I love you so much but how could I declare.
You're the one for me, and I won't walk away I swear.
Can you handle all the pain from me?
I know you can because you'll set it free.
My heart inside tells me to stay with you.
I pray to God you can break this spell; yes I do.
I want to know what you're going to do with the spell.
It can make your heaven maybe a hell.
I hope you know the answer; please say it today.
Do you want to leave or stay?

These Quarrels Make No Sense.

When People start fighting.
It's all because the words aren't colliding.
What is all the fighting for?
Don't you know it can hurt your partner only more?
Don't make the problems to deep.
Make sure that the problems are solved before you go to sleep.
The feelings you're piling up inside.
Let it out before it's to late and please don't hide.
These quarrels make no sense at all.
You don't want to let your relationship fall.
People talk it out, before it's to late, or you'll have regrets of what
you've said.
Always remember of the good things of the love ones instead.
Open up yourself to your partner and bring the love back.
Don't go away and get lost but follow the same track.
Cherish and carry every moment like a glove.
Be honest and truthful towards the one you love.

Now It's Time For Me To Open My Eyes.

Today I was sitting and thinking about the way I live.
Thinking to myself why do people always take and never give.
I try to keep myself pure and complete.
It's feels like I'm being beat.
I try hard to make people smile.
I just need a break for a little while.
Sometimes it feels like things are coming to a stop.
Then I turn around, I feel like I'm spinning like a top.
My mind and my words are clear.
Seems all I do is shed a tear.
I try to help so many people if I could.
Some people aren't there for me like they should.
Sometimes my life feels like my friends aren't there.
For now I really don't even care.
It's time for me to open my eyes.
Watch who really is telling me lies.
I made my heart cold as ice.
Then People can't throw my feelings around like dice.
I'm trying to be strong.
I know I'm not always wrong.
Well here are my feelings put down in front of you.
I chance my life and now it's totally new.

Baby I Love You So.

I love her so bad she's my precious baby.
Our love is so strong and tight lately.
My heart pounds when she comes in my sight.
My body starts to shake with all its might.
I start to sweat and pull her to my skin.
Hoping that she wants me deep within.
I start to stroke and kiss her lips.
As I feel her reaching for my hips.
I raised her arms and pull her blouse over her head.
I'll lay her down; baby I want you so bad, I said.
She started to move and moan in my ear.
Then I heard her say, please baby come here.
I asked her do you want to feel me deep inside of you.
She moaned to me and said, yes baby I do.
We came to the point where there was no return.
We both are so excited that we could feel an erotic burn.
With desire I screamed her name.
While she act exactly the same.
We both came towards our climax together.
All I wanted is to hold her tight forever.
I asked God, never chance the way we are inside.
This feeling we have, we don't want it to hide.
This is love that I'll never let stray away.
Baby I love you forever and a day.

My Love Is Pure And God Already Knew

Love to feel your hands through my hair.
I'm in love with you and for the rest I don't care.
What I feel for you I can't explain.
When I see or hear you my heart goes fast like a train.
I don't need someone else cause you're the air that I respire.
You're so good for me you're love is my hearts desire.
You tell you're love to my heart every day.
Your eyes tell it all; you really don't need any words to say.
Hopefully this poem will open your feeling so you understand.
When you touch my face all I want to do is hold your hand.
My love is pure and God already knew this.
He brought us back together by just a single kiss.
The time is passing quick for our eternal time together.
I won't hesitate to marry you and be a family man forever.

Just Listen To Your Heart.

I'm lonely when you're not around.
Then I feel lost and I can't be found.
Sometimes I try to go into a town.
But without you all I do is frown.
All I do is think how much I'm missing you.
My heart starts to slow down like its old and not new.
I don't like the feeling inside of me.
Emptiness and sorrow isn't what it should be.
I want to hold you and never let you go.
I'll hold so tight; and she said I know.
I'll give you all of me this is what I'll do.
When you want more just take my hand and pull me to you.
We're so far away from each other.
We have a fear; will there be another?
Just listen to your heart.
So we'll never get torn apart.
We both have a love that's so strong.
No one can come between us, because that would be wrong.
Your my heart my soul your blood is running through my vein.
It feels so good but not like a pain.
This is pure love.
Sent to us from heaven above.
As lovers and friends we're bound together.
This is only a beginning and it will last forever.

I'll Always Remember The Day You're Gone.

Inside I cry for you now that you're past away.
The feeling of crying is so strong these days.
I'll miss you now that the angels took you to a better place.
I have a picture of you in my heart so I'll never forget your face.
You'll be always in my heart no matter where I go.
But at this moment I'm lost and I need my friends also.
Hold me now I'm down and alone these days.
I can't believe you're past away.
This poem is ment for people that lost some one.
It's hard and never fun.
We need support from our friends and family.
They understand the feeling inside of me.
Here are my words to the person that passed away.
I'll always remember you on our best and funniest day.
I'll always remember the day you're gone.
By playing that day our special song.
I'll pray you find your peace in heaven above.
When you look down remember the people who you love.
One day I'll see you again when it's my time to come.
And it will be like old days with laughter and fun.
Don't wait for me but be there when I arrive.
Then we're together for an eternal life.

Memories Will Always Be There.

I know soon I'll say goodbye.
Then there you go to the angels in the sky.
Last thing you said sound very sad.
It makes my heart cry very bad.
You just want to go home where you belong.
Sometime I sense your presents even when I know you're gone.
The person you are.
Is like a shining star.
It's sad though; now you're away.
You'll stay in my heart every day.
Time goes fast.
When I looked into the past.
Memories will always be there.
Sometime life isn't fair.
Seeing you so ill before your die.
Inside my body I just wanted to cry.
Wish I could heal you from your pain.
My tears keep falling like rain.
I prayed to God every day.
Just to let you sleep so you could fly away.
It's hard to watch you take your last breath of air.
When you closed you're eyes: I thanked you for the moments we
were able to share.

Being A Victim Of A Bully Isn't Nice.

To bring someone down to his or her knees is not a good start.
It's so easy to tear a person completely apart.
How can I stop it I have no clue.
This feeling is hurting me; I cry inside what must I do?
Why am I a victim I'm not someone's bait.
When the bullies come back it's all too late.
Being a victim of a bully isn't nice.
They always pick on me not once but twice.
Nowhere too run or hide tonight.
I'm scared cause I don't like to fight.
I was always lucky to hear the school bell.
When school was over I'd ran home like hell.
One bully is no problem more is like a nightmare.
Crying and wishing they'd leave me alone cause it wasn't fair.
I never told this at home but my mom just knew.
I was afraid I didn't know what to do.
Finally I concur my fears.
It took a lot of years.
You think all things would chance?
It didn't cause fear is still in my veins.
There're days I still feel the fear.
All I do then is cry with a tear.

Today Is The Big Day

Today I'm going to marry with the love of my life.
We're walking together to the altar and soon she'll be my wife.
A long fairytale is coming truth today.
I'm very nervous and don't know what to say.
To place this ring on your finger makes my heart pound.
The choir sings gospel God I love that sound.
Everything is perfect through out this day.
There're no clouds or rain only the suns ray.
A lot of people are coming to the wedding party to night.
It will be crazy I going to hold my heart tight.
The bands playing all kinds of music we like.
With a surprise I ask for the mic.
I started with a poem; then I'll sing a song with the band.
I gave you my heart my soul and today I give you my hand.
Baby I love you! And nothing will go wrong.
Because the love I have for you is that strong.
I'll marry you because I want to be a family man from today.
We'll be happy till the day we'll die; that's my final prayer I'll say.
Come here Baby and hold me close and never let go of me.
I love you from the first day we met and now till eternity.

A Wish Comes True

When I think about you.
I think about a fairytale coming true.
Love and happiness is all I see.
Sorrow and pain is not for me.
I'll give you a future with hope.
My love is so strong I hope you can cope.
For right now I have my dreams.
But lately that's not enough so it seems.
My heart tells me I'm coming there my dear.
I know this is true I see it clear.
When you see me walking off the plane.
Your heart will go completely insane.
I know you'll run and come to me fast.
Never let go baby I want it to last.
Then we'll go to the car for a ride.
And I'll come sit by your side.
The trip to our home wasn't so bad.
When we came home everyone was glad.
My baby's family greeted me like a king from the start.
I made her feel like she's my princes or even my queen of my heart.
So see my dear readers, see what this could be.
A fairytale comes true but not only for me.

A Year Went By So Fast

The truth is that I'll always love you.
It doesn't matter what you say or do.
The whole world may know how I feel.
My heart is not made of steel.
Baby you're always on my mind.
This time I wont leave you behind.
I fell in love with you the first time I saw you.
Now! I can't help myself God what must I do.
My heart belongs to you; just give me the chance to show you love.
It's not weird that we met again it's because of the help from the angels above.
I can't believe a year went by so fast.
Soon we're together forever last.
Just a little more time is all we need.
Few more months and then we meet.
Deep in my heart I know I'll never go away.
I can't! I love you and your son more and more each day.
So smile for us and pray and you'll see.
That God will help us till eternity.
This love is sent by the Lord I know this from my heart.
The Lord wants us back together and not broken apart.

Run And Hide Away

Many fears so I run and hide away.
This feeling was getting dreadful every day.
With bruises and marks I came home and run to my bed.
For days I didn't eat but stayed in my room instead.
I didn't want to go back to school.
My mom said, don't be a fool!
She didn't know what happen to me.
Till she seen the bruises on my body and knee.
It was a bump is all I said, it don't hurt bad.
I didn't want to have my mom upset or mad.
I came home with a bloody nose and a black and blue eye.
My mom asks what happen but I didn't replay.
She tries to talk but all I did was run and hide.
Then I set in a corner and cried with pain inside.
One day she followed me to school and back.
Then she had seen the bullies on my track.
She was angry and went to the school principal and talked about
me.
She said there are some kids that are bad and hurting her son
constantly
Finally my mom helped me to concur my fears.
She brought me to laughter and took away my tears.

It's Your Love

I want to dance with you in the middle of the night.
Listen to your heart while I hold you very tight.
You gave me a passionate touch.
Baby I love you so much.
I ask you to never let me go.
It's your love that makes it so.
Love is a beautiful thing.
The feelings I have for you, I can't hold it within.
You ask cause you wonder.
What kind of spell are you under?
Then I would say it your love it does something to me.
It's like a shock that's runs through me, baby cant you see?
The person that I'm now is the one I want to be inside.
You made this happen; you said let out your feeling, don't you hide!
The person I was before I met you, I don't want to be!
Your love makes it all better it makes me happy and free.
All the changes that happen to me, I owe it to you.
Even when you call out my name, that's all you have to do.
I told you it's all because of your love.
That brings me to the 7th heaven above.

The Girl Who Made Me Stronger

My girl sets and listens to me; when I talked about my past.
It made her see that I couldn't walk I had to run fast.
Some people in this cold world are mean.
When we open our hearts it could be filled with sunshine and
gleam.
She told me it would be ok now.
I said; but baby its deep and it wont come out no how.
Together we'll concur all fears.
We'll wash away all of your tears.
She said you're a good man now you'll take your stand.
In this cold world you'll be the strongest man.
The people will now see.
All they did was made you stronger and free.
All you'll need to do is put the past to rest.
Come out and be the man we all knew is best.
I'll stand by your side.
No matter what decision you ever decide.
I love you baby forever and a day.
You'll see nothing can break us no way.
I thank the girl that made me stronger in life.
She's not only my friend she's my lover and also my wife.

Words On A Disk

Kids at school laughed at me because I written words as poetry.
How could they be so cruel? It's just a part of me.
While the sun shined on my face.
My mind drifts of to that special place.
It happened every time I set against a tree.
All I did was write words about the feelings inside of me.
I had a chance to use the computer at school.
I printed out the words and some people say; wow! Your poetry is cool.
I said; they're just some words in my head how I feel today.
The words come easy to me; that's why I write it down this way.
Some say, why don't you make a book?
All I did was stare to them with a strange look.
I save all the words on a disk so I could work with it at home.
I always did this when I was alone.
My mom found the papers and came to me.
She asks did you write this poetry?
I said; yes I write everything with my own words and hand.
She said; it's all English and it hard for me to understand.
I translate the words to Dutch and all she said was; it's sound like poetry to me.
Maybe you'll grow up as the biggest poet in history.

Somewhere Over The Rainbow

Somewhere over the rainbow what lays there for me.
Happiness or sorrow, well I'll wait and see.
A pot of gold isn't what I'm looking for.
I ask for a heart full of love I don't need more.
When I see a rainbow in the sky.
I'll make a wish for you and I.
A rainbow has many colors and its pretty to see.
It's like the love that's destined for you and me.
When you see a rainbow touch the clouds, close then your eyes.
Make a wish it will come true when you still see that rainbow in
the sky.
There's for everyone a girl or a boy.
Let your heart go and feel the joy.
A rainbow caught my eye.
When the birds were singing in the sky.
To love someone that's a wish from me.
And to be with my baby! for eternally.
To love her with a love so warm that would be wild.
To be a proud father that looks at his newborn child.
I want to give my love to someone special in my life.
Under a rainbow I want to ask her: baby do you want to be my wife?

You're A Dream Come True.

It's almost unreal.
This love that we both feel.
You're so deep in my skin.
You're love I carry deep within.
I'll let no one change the way I feel.
My love for you is like a wall of steel.
From the first day I already knew.
Yet People Just didn't understand why I loved you.
It's the love that I felt through your eyes.
Now I'm floating on cloud nine to a new paradise.
I'll leave my past behind.
Three times it has to be a sign.
I'll do everything just to be with you.
I'll even walk twice through hell to show you I do.
I don't do it just for you yet also for our little son.
It's also his love and his inspiration.
The things I do I'll do it for the both of you.
You're a dream that has come true.
I know we're far apart at this moment in our life.
When we're together I won't hesitate to ask you to be my wife.

I Don't Want To Leave Her

This year it feels like we're having tropical weather.
I wish it would rain then I'd stand right under it to feel better.
It's like a heat wave coming this way.
For a long time there's no rain during the day.
Theirs many people at the beach or in a pool.
The sun is hot but I like the water it's nice and cool.
I never felt this heat in summers before.
My best friend calls me and say's; do you want to spend a day on
the shore.
I never went to the shore cause I don't leave my girl behind.
People say; you have only one thing on your mind.
I'd rather take a shower now and then so I'd cool down.
Then be somewhere else with a frown.
I don't want to leave the one I love alone on the Internet.
I don't mind how wet I'll be from my sweat.
I never felt like this before.
I don't want to leave her I just want more.
Her love is pure and that's why I can't leave.
She's my sun and the air that I breathe.
I won't mind how warm it will be.
No one will push her away from me.
I know no one understands me but I don't care.
I'll give everything up just to see the sunshine in her hair.

Work It Out

A relationship is about taken and giving.
Staying mad is the wrong way of living.
Always work it out before you go to sleep; cause you know.
The Pain and anger is wrong when you don't let it go.
Yelling and shouting doesn't solve a problem at all.
It's bad when you want to see your partner fall.
Who is changing here cause I'm in fear?
I'll hope it's not you my dear.
We'll work it out in some kind of way.
Not tomorrow or next week but today!
Where did it start what's the fact.
Is there a reason why you think and react?
I want to work it out baby cause it only hurts me inside.
I know at this moment our words don't collide.
They say true love makes you blind.
You're always in my dreams and on my mind.
I didn't listen to you and that was wrong.
Please don't go cause my love for you is strong.
Come in my arms, we'll work this out.
We love each other and that's all its about.

I Want To Thank Author House Publishers

The first step is completed I'm on the road as a well know poet.
My heart pounds fast of joy you just don't know it.
To see my name in a book that people will read everywhere.
I show the world my feelings that I want to share.
This is the first time my work is published in a book.
I was so amazed when I took a look.
When I heard my poems going into a book I cried.
My emotions where running wild and I couldn't hide.
To see some work of my own I never dream of this.
I showed the book to my mom she hug me and gave me a kiss.
She said wow! That book is great and nice.
She had noticed the tears in my eyes when she looked twice.
Now my name will be recognized everywhere.
I told my friends see my name is in there.
People on the street ask me; why are you so happy today?
I'll show them the book, that's why I said (in a happy way).
Why did you start to write poetry they ask?
All I could say was God gave me this task.
I thank Author House for their time and effort they give to me.
Cause they believed in me, and the way I write my poetry.

My Name Is Werner And This Is My Story

I'm a male from 1977.
My girl said that I'm a gift from heaven.
My life had lots of fears.
But we all have good and bad years.
My girl said; I have a Romantic touch with my words and eyes.
There's one thing I don't like it's when people tell me lies.
I like music mostly of all kind.
I know a lot of movie quotes out of my mind.
People ask don't you get tired of your personality?
I don't care what people think, I don't chance I just being me.
Love to party and drink with good friends.
I love to write my poetry and hope it never ends.
I ride my bike every day.
To my work or the city I'm always on my way.
I like to go shopping in the mall.
I'm five foot seven and I feel very tall.
Love to ride roller coasters in a park.
But I'm scared when I ride alone in the dark.
This is the way I am and I'm not ashamed to tell you.
I write poetry so you can feel love, pain, and happiness to.

The Things I Do

What must I say?
I did something wrong today.
What should I do to make it right?
I'm going to sit here and gaze at the moonlight.
Wondering where did I go wrong.
Damn! My love is so strong.
Girl I never wanted to hurt you.
My love for you is so true.
I wish you knew what you ment to me.
I want to marry you some day you'll see.
Time is what its all about.
Though I'm sad I never cry out loud.
Everyday when I speak to you.
You turn my darkest day clear blue.
I want to embrace you so close and tight.
To make this feeling all right.
I don't want to let you go.
I think I must go a little bit slow.
You said; I'm a little different in a way.
But the things I do for you, you'll love it every day.
With music I show you how I feel.
Till you understand that my love for you is real.
We just need time for the two of us.
Let's do it slow so we won't rush.

The Mask

Hiding behind a mask.
That wasn't such a difficult task.
I perform in a way I didn't want to be.
I was wearing a mask, people thought it was the real me.
Hiding behind a mask was a hell of a mess.
It was not easy I must confess.
All I did was hide the way I feel.
By wearing a mask of steel.
The mask changed the whole inside of me.
I was crying behind it because I wasn't free.
When I'm with my girlfriend I'll never wear my mask.
Just be yourself is all she ask.
It's funny that I never used the mask when I met you.
I was myself something I hardly ever do.
You know me as a person in real.
From that moment I threw away the mask of steel.
For you I'll never chance back to the way I was before.
Cause I don't need the mask no more.
The love that you give me makes me see.
That I'm the person you love inside out and that's the way I want
to be.

You're Back In My Life

I met an American woman she's so good to me.
She said to me do you want to be free.
I never felt love this kind of way.
So sad we're far apart and that's why I miss her every day.
When I saw her eyes on the very first night.
I was stun and paralyzed when my eyes cross her sight.
I thought I'd never see her back in my life for a second time.
We met again and the love we made was so fine.
Wish the second time we could change what happened that day.
Then I would stay but instead I walked away.
So again we lost each other sight.
And then came God and he show us the light.
On the Internet we met after five years.
Now we're waiting to be together while we cry every day heavily
tears.
It still amazes me that you're back in my life.
I'll give you everything, even my heart I would cut it out with a
knife.
My love for you is more then true.
I dedicate all my love for you two.
It won't be long before we're together.
There's no women who could give me love the way you do
"forever"!

She Missed Me

My girl misses me so much.
She longed for my soft touch.
I was working at a new job today.
She missed me more then she really would say.
As I came back from work I said hi baby I'm home.
She looked at me when she heard my soft tone.
I walked to her and she asks how was your first day?
I told her I can work on my on pace and the people are okay.
She said; I watched the clock that turns with the moment of time.
But now you're home and I'm completely fine.
I didn't know she would be so happy to see me.
She reached out her hand and stroked my face very slowly.
She said, baby I missed you all day long.
I started to cry is that so wrong?
Even though the tears were coming down my face.
I put a happy smile on so she wouldn't see any trace.
I missed you to darling I must not lie.
At my break I thought of you while my eyes filled with tears to cry.
Work went very well today.
I learned a lot I must say.
We don't worry about the time, because it doesn't really matter.
It's weekend! Now it's time for us together.

Essence Of Love

Give your love with all your heart.
Also when your love one is far apart.
Love isn't about age or height.
Sometime you find love on first sight.
This feels like deja vu.
Does that give you a clue?
What is love all about?
For me it's to love your partner inside out.
Love has no lust.
Give your partner instead 100 % trust.
Don't try to chance your mate.
Sometime love is destined by fate.
Don't try to change your love or let your feelings hide.
Let the one you love inside.
What is the essence of love?
To be with your angel that God has sent from heaven above.
Love isn't a light that you can turn out.
So think to your self what is love all about?
Every one makes decisions in there own way.
You don't have to do what I say.
I give you advice so do what you must do.
The end decisions are all up to you.
I hope you will see.
That love can be unconditionally.

Beaten

I know a woman that's been beat up by her man.
What's the reason cause I really don't understand?
In the beginning everything was okay.
It just suddenly changed in one day.
To beat up a woman to get sex is just not a right thing to do.
What was the purpose I really don't have a clue.
She's very afraid she didn't feel free.
Her feelings say it's no love what I feel cause he disgusts me.
She said to me, in one week I'm going to divorce and sue.
I said to her; is this what you really want to do?
Then two day's later I heard her man beat her very bad.
I went to the hospital she looked sad but inside she was mad.
She said; I really want this divorce this is what I want to do.
He didn't only beat me but he cheated to.
I don't want to live this life with him no more.
I don't like to be beaten to the floor.
I said okay I would help you as best that I can.
You mean more to me then a friend I wanted I to be your man.
Yet I never told you before what I truly felt inside.
I was in love with but the feelings for you I had to hide.
She said to bad I never married you.
Cause deep in my heart I loved you to.

Writing A Poem Outside A Café

Poetry is just a part of me.
I write with my feeling to set myself free.
I'm sitting by a café outside.
The sun is hot so in the shadows I'll hide.
Looking at the people as they walk by.
I see couples walking hand in hand and inside I cry.
At this moment my love one is far away.
To see people happy together hurts my heart every day.
I'm living here in The Netherlands and she's from the USA.
I'm sitting here and my coffee is getting cold and my mind drifts
far away.
Before I set down by this café I looked for English poetry.
Go to the big city there you'll find it people said to me.
I ordered a second cup of coffee and waited for one hour to past by.
You'll ask me of course why?
I turned in a roll of film and in an hour it should be done.
That's why I sip on some coffee in the shadows and out of the sun.
I walked through the stores in this street and now I'm beat.
I have all my groceries all piled and neat.
An hour has past.
Now I can get my pictures at last.
I'll pay for my coffee and I'll head for home.
I'll work on my poetry all alone.

My Own Way

To write poetry isn't easy some days.
Every body writes it in their own ways.
I prefer to write with my soul and heart.
Some people say I'm unique and smart.
I care what people say.
I write poetry in my own way.
I never use much of my mind.
For me the words aren't hard to find.
Words come to me when I'm in a crowd or on my own.
I work my words out to a poem when I'm at home.
In the past I threw the words I written away.
I'm still mad at myself cause I could use them today.
I write even more then before.
It always starts in the morning when I step out of bed on to the
floor.
I really enjoy writing.
To know that people read my poems that's exciting.
My life without poetry I can't Image no more.
I express feelings of people and love ones I adore.
I write what I feel, see or hear.
My story's goes in to poems about happiness, trust, family,
friends, and fear.
I've written my poetry in different genre so people would
remember them for years.
My friend's say when they read my poems they would smile
tremble and shed tears.
By talking and discussing with people brings words to my mind.
I want to show you by reading my poetry there's a new world to
find.

Genie (Part One)

I found a genie in a lamp and he told me.
I can grant you wishes but only three.
And there are rules you can't break.
He said I hope you understand and please make no mistake.
Rule 1 I will not kill.
Rule 2 I can't do nothing about free will.
Rule 3 I won't bring dead people back to the living that's not a
nice thing to do.
Rule 4 you can't wish for more wishes; three is all I can give to you.
So I'll let you think of the three wishes the genie said.
I was thinking so hard it was hurting my head.
Wish one wasn't so hard I wished everyone happiness forever.
He said it will be done, and he snapped his fingers together.
The second wish was to give luck to all the people who are in need.
The genie said that's a great wish indeed.
Last wish I didn't think twice it was very easy for me.
Then I said genie I wish you free.
He cry and said; no one had wished a genie free before.
While the wish was spoken his shackles felt to the floor.
You're my best friend said the genie and I owe you my life till
eternity.
Because you where the person that set me free.

Stay In The Hospital

You're in a hospital cause you're very unwell.
Girl you making me cry and my eyes start to swell.
Wish you would take care of your illness.
I miss you I must confess.
You have to promise me to get your strength up and come back
home.
Without you I'll die cause I'd feel so alone.
Why don't you listen to me when you don't feel well?
You're now very sick and I really can tell.
I knew that you weren't feeling well or strong.
Why did you let your illness go on for so long?
You didn't go to the doctor I know this for sure.
I wanted you to feel better and maybe he had the cure.
I know what I'm going to say isn't fair.
Baby you have to stay in the hospital right there.
I worry more then you think.
Life is precious just like an eye blink.
You should have gone to the doctor but you made the wrong choice.
Now you're in the hospital and there is no rejoice.
You better take the time to go the doctor that you need.
Not seeing you for days make my heart just bleed.
Please get better as soon as you can.
Then you'll be back with your son and your man.

The Teacher Knew

At school I knew a guy.
In the class he was very shy.
He was always silent in the class.
The reasons why? Is because his father kicked his ass.
He told this to no one.
God who would beat up his own daughter or son?
Fear was in his eyes.
He created his own words by telling lies.
One day our teacher found out about that he was mistreated.
His teacher got on the phone he screamed, shout and pleaded.
He told the father of the child he was mad.
What he had done to his son was very bad.
If I find out you beat your child again! I'll call the police right away.
I saw that little child choke up and freeze and he didn't know
what to say.
Days later he came in the classroom with a bruise close by his
forehead hairs.
He told the teacher that he tripped on his shoelace and fell down
from the stairs.
But the teacher knew something was wrong and called the police.
The teacher said for you safety I'll send you home with my niece.
Day's later the teacher told us he was brought to a new family.
The whole class wrote him a letter he replied; I feel happy and free.
I'll never forget his shy little face.
Last thing I remember is I heard he moved to a new place.

Four Seasons Of Loneliness

I have four seasons of loneliness.
I want to see you I want to feel your kiss.
The winter without you is so cold.
You're not near I want you to hold.
What about spring?
It's for most people a life with a new song to sing.
The trees are getting greener by the day.
The weather gets warmer at the first sunray.
Then summer comes around the corner and summertime will begin.
I avoid the hot sun; so I jump in the water and take a swim.
I dislike hot summer heat.
In the meantime I miss your heartbeat.
The days are passing by so fast.
Seasons fly by and they don't last.
Fall is here I'm seeing the colors on the leaves.
The nights are getting colder and I feel the breeze.
Slowly the nights get longer.
Our love grows stronger.
You're the one that I miss.
With in the four seasons of loneliness.

Fly Home

I wish I could fly.
Just as a bird through the sky.
Or float through the air.
The wind will take me everywhere.
It would be amazing to dream this some day.
Just spread your wings and fly away.
Feeling the wind through the feathers of my wing.
How would it feel? I guest very amazing.
In real people aren't able to fly.
But a plane will take us to the sky.
I'll stop with dreams and fantasize.
Soon I fly to my paradise.
I know I'll fly home some night.
When my heart and soul feels right.
Through every kind of weather I would fly to you.
It's because our love is strong I know you would do the same thing
to.
I'll be there soon in your sight.
For you I'll fly day and night.
Like a mother who'll protect her little ones under her wings today.
I'll do the same to you I'll pull you to me without a word to say.

Rhythm Of Our Beating Heart

Lying next to you.
That's what I want to do.
I love you so much.
You turn me on with your touch.
My hands are going through your hair.
I'll kiss you everywhere.
A passion touch and kiss on your lips.
Stroking slowly towards your hips.
Your skin is so soft like silk and warm as fire.
Girl you get me burning with desire.
You know the places that turn me on even more.
Making love slowly while we hear the favorite songs we adore.
I love to tease you very long.
Slowly you take off my thong.
Kissing your privet part.
I hear the rhythm of your beating heart.
Coming close together in and out.
I don't mind what neighbors think I love it when you moan and
shout.
After we made love I held you tight.
Honey you show me what love is all about day and night.

Forever In My Heart

I'm writing this poem to tell you that I love you.
Last night I cried all night through.
I don't want you to give up on me.
I'll be with you just wait and see.
We all can lose love in a blink of an eye.
We're stronger than that, besides without you I'd die.
Sometimes life isn't what it supposes to be.
We know for sure this love is ment for you and me.
Our love is pure as solid gold.
We belong together till we die old.
Every day is a brand new day.
God knows what's coming our way.
My love for you stays the same.
In my head I hear your name.
God forbids something to happen and we part.
You'll be the one till I die; forever you're in my heart.
There's no one that loves me like you do.
Your love is pure soft and incredibly true.
I'll not love someone new in life; you're the one for me.
I hope I made you understand; my love for you is for eternity.

School Break

There she is walking down the street.
When I look at her I feel my heart start to beat.
I'm afraid to tell her how I feel.
She doesn't look at me! So does she know I'm real?
I'm a misfit of the school.
It hurts me, why are people so cruel.
I want to say something to her but I start to shake.
I always turn red when she looks at me during school break.
Does she like me to? Wish I had a clue.
She's the most popular girl at school I knew.
She blushes when I look in her eyes.
Tomorrow I'll take a chance to ask her out I wonder if that's wise?
I got to be strong and show her what my feelings are.
I'm walked to her and said: your eyes look like a bright star.
Girl may I ask you do you believe in fate?
If you don't mind would you join me for a date?
I want to take you to a movie after a dinner for two.
I'll ask this cause I have an eye for you.
I was waiting for her answer hopefully she wouldn't say no.
With a big surprise she said; I love to cause I have feeling for you
also.

My Heart Asks For You

Love is more then words to me.
It's all about the feelings inside, you see?
I feel the butterflies in my belly.
Feelings of real love make me mushy like jelly.
When you're truly in love you never leave your partner alone.
Being in love make you strong like stone.
Love is like a river.
Its fast and slow and it makes you quiver.
Her smile is bright like the sun in the sky.
I'm in love and it feels like I can fly.
You're the one that my heart asks for.
For me it doesn't matter if she's rich or poor.
And when she doesn't understand.
Don't doubt my love when I ask for her hand.
Did she know her name resounds in my head?
When I'm not with her I'm feeling very sad.
I said to her; come here darling and hold me tight.
So we can sit and under the dazzling moon tonight.
When we're together and I'm close to my girl.
Loving her is all I want do, she's my precious pearl.

Holding On To Your Love

I woke up this morning with you in my head.
I saw the pretty sunshine even though I was sad.
My heart is hurting for you my love; cause you're not here.
That's why I don't have too much to cheer.
I know love is hard to hold on to.
I hold your love in my heart cause I know our love is true.
Sometimes you scare me with the words you say.
Like yesterday I cried all day.
We love each other this is true.
Separation makes lovers very blue.
I want you to know I'll wait for you.
I can only pray you'll wait for me to.
It's hard without that real touch.
Baby! Please remember that I love you so much.
Don't have doubts you know what to do.
Hold on to me I'm always here for you.
Our life together will be perfect some day.
I ask the Lord; please listen to me when I pray.
So sweetheart hold on to my love real tight.
Don't let us leave nor lose each other's sight.
We'll be together just wait and you'll see.
You and I were ment to be.

That Special Place

I'll take you back in time and space.
Were we met each other at that special place.
This time we can change what happen before.
Let's go back to the place we adore.
Sitting back on the sundeck on the same boat.
You got the chills so I gave you my coat.
Baby we're back at the same place.
I still remember the first time when I seen your face.
Love was found right here do you remember?
It was before the month of November.
We see the boat its back again waiting by the shore.
It lets our hearts beat even more.
We're walking to our cabin together this time.
This trip will be awesome and completely fine.
Here I have a memory of seeing your face.
Never thought we'd be back at the same place.
I love you baby and this time I'm with you.
I'll cherries this trip completely through.
Come in my arms my precious dear.
This time I can hold you the whole trip near.

Not Only The Love

When I make Love with you.
That's my decision when I do.
I know you're a heavy girl.
But you rock my world.
You set me on fire.
Your kisses are a sweet touch of heavenly desire.
Even though you're heavyset.
I love you from the moment we met.
The shaking from your heavy body drives me wild.
Baby in my heart you're the one and also your child.
It's not only the love between us.
Your characteristics are the biggest plus.
You're funny, kind, and romantic to.
There are so many reasons why I love you.
I don't care what people say.
My love for you gets stronger every day.
For me it was love at first sight.
I know you feel the same way, right?
The first kiss brought me to heaven up in space.
Looking in your eyes makes me want to touch your face.

I Am Someone

I thank heaven that I met you.
It turned my gray world blue.
You let me be the person I am inside.
She told me baby don't let yourself hide.
It was you that helped me out of hell.
Usually I'm not a shy guy in a shell.
I picked up my life that I hid for so long.
You let me believe that I'm strong.
My feelings for you, I can show them now.
In the past I couldn't figure out how.
I can say I know this is love that I feel.
Now I don't have to hide behind a mask of steel.
I'll show you a sign that lights up your road ahead.
I can teach you how to keep people of your back she said.
Even though when I'm serious or when we're have a lot of fun.
She lead's me to believe that I am someone.
I've picked up again my poetry.
That I've hid for so long inside of me.
I thanked her for all she has done.
She made me feel happy like I'm a special someone.

Talk With Experience

I love making love with you.
Its more amazing then I ever knew.
A heavy person makes better love its true.
I can't get enough from you.
Your love is pure like rain.
Your kiss is like a shock it drive me insane.
Girl you rock my heaven and earth.
You're so great to me I promise there will be no hurt.
I love to see her body move when she is excited.
It turns me on when she moans and she can't hide it.
Once a heavy person gives love to you.
It will be forever and true.
I talk with experience about this.
I already had her touch and kiss.
My girl is heavy but she loves me unconditionally.
She gave me her heart and soul forever and eternally.
I love her with my whole heart.
She pleases me right from the start.
I'll never let her go out of my life.
Marry me baby, because I want you to be my wife.

What Would It Take?

A relationship is great.
I know our love is fate.
I knew we had doubts in the past.
All the doubts are now worked out forever it last.
There's one thing in my mind that makes me understand.
That is I love you, I want to be your man.
What would it take?
Before a heart would break.
My heart will die when you're away.
I'd miss you and stay alone, forever and a day.
When I found you, it was like a roll of the dice.
You make me feel like we're in paradise.
When you were out of my sight.
I'd cried day and night.
I love you more then life.
Let us marry, girl do you want to be my wife?
I'd give everything so we would never part.
Cause girl! You've gained my soul and heart.
I have so much love for you inside of me.
I'll never leave you; my love is like a flame that burns for eternity.

Lying Next To Me

What will we do when the morning comes along?
I can hear the birds chirping their own little song.
I woke up with the morning glory.
Every person has his or her own story.
Seeing you lying close to me in bed.
On my chest there's your head.
My fingertips touch your body and face.
I'll make love with you at a slowly pace.
I was waiting for this moment for so long.
I'm watching you crawl to me while the radio plays a song.
It feels so good you lying next to me.
This is now life and no fantasy.
You're looking into my eyes.
While you said, am I in paradise?
I replied, baby this is real we're together.
It will be like this forever.
So come in my arms real close and tight.
Finally you're by my side and in my sight.
We'll give love to our children together.
And be a happy family forever.

I Treasure Our Love

I love you more then I can say.
First time I saw you again it felt like yesterday.
Memories never erase.
Wish we could go back to that time and place.
Our love is still the same.
Only now I know your name.
This love we share.
Is unique and rare.
I won't let you go.
Instead I'll give my love slow.
Both of us had a broken heart, but never any more.
This love inside of us; we never felt it before.
Ever minute of the day I treasure our love.
That's why I thank the Lord in heaven above.
Not only you have taken my heart.
Also your son took an equal part.
He accepts me like his daddy.
For a family life, I'm ready.
This I know for sure.
I won't to give up on you any more.

A Special Bond

I've written some words so you know; I never run away.
Our hearts are joined as one forever and a day.
I love you so much I only pray you understand.
My love for you grows continuous and grand.
Every day I'll let you see.
That my love I have for you is for eternity.
I never knew I could feel this way.
I thank the Lord for you ever night when I pray.
I never had a real love and it makes me sad.
The Lord sent me an angel in you, now I'm very glad.
I dream about you when I close my eyes.
I love to drift off with you to a newfound paradise.
You give me more love than I ever had before.
I want to take a walk with you by the seashore.
When we lay down I touch your skin.
I'll kiss you with passion when I'm lifting your chin.
You and I have a special bond with each other.
Our love is to strong, to be broken by another.
You and I will stay forever young.
Cause our hearts beat together like a song.

Pay No Attention To The Time

When I'm with you.
My heart pounds for two.
When I lay next to you in our bed.
Sexy thoughts and dreams run through my head.
I love you so much.
I hunger for your touch.
I roll over toward you and watch your smile.
I hope you wake up just for a little while.
Then I'll kiss you on your neck with my lips.
Tenderly you stroked my body and hips.
You start to touch me in places I never would guess.
Baby when you touch me you make me feel so blessed.
I see a smile come over your face.
I like it when you touch that special place.
Then you feel my hands slowly going down your skin.
I know you want to make love you want me in.
Making love with you is always so fine.
Come here my love and pay no attention to the time.
Take me fast or even slow.
Any way you want to go.
When you and I make passionate love.
We drift off to heaven above.

Heart Is Broken

This morning I woke up and felt so bad.
I was crying the whole night damn I feel sad.
My heart is broken in millions parts and shattered all over the floor.
Cause my love one walked yesterday right out the door.
She said; that our love didn't work out and it has to end.
She doesn't want to see me any more, not even as a friend.
What went wrong between us?
She didn't say very much.
It feels like I disappeared into the ground.
She walked away with her things and never made a sound.
I went for a walk alone to the park.
It was cold and raven dark.
She never told me why she had ended our love.
I was thinking about it, while looking to the stars in the sky above.
God knows why this is the way.
From that moment I had a special prayer to say.
Please God let me find love that's ment to be.
A person that is equal and right for me.
I want a person that loves me more then life it self every day.
Amen to God! For he listened to my prayer I had to say.

Hidden Feelings

Out of England there comes this guy.
He's funny and makes me laugh and cry.
His heart is solid gold that's unique for a man.
For some people it's hard to understand.
He never told people how he feels inside.
There was a loving feeing that he tried to hide.
I know the Englishman hides a special love.
It's my Internet brother he's such an angel from above.
That's why my lady and I plot a plan.
I do it all for love for my brother and the Englishman.
I told how my brother loves the man out of the U.K.
In my heart I knew this love would be okay.
I told the Englishman to follow his heart and mind.
The person he loves would give him a sign.
We threw a net party and both of them ended up drunk that night.
We all know a drunken person will revile feeling without a fight.
With an amazing shock the Englishman opened his heart and soul.
He was drunk so his feeling came out and he wasn't in control.
He asked my brother to marry him.
God put them together he knew it was no sin.

I Feel Bad Inside

Yesterday I acted in the wrong way.
I felt bad about it the whole next day.
My words weren't so kind.
Girl you know I always speak my mind.
I don't like to fight.
We both know it's not right.
It's hard not to fight when things inside bottle up and don't drop.
I was so angry and my words didn't stop.
Baby I don't want to hurt you.
That is the last thing that I wanted to do.
Girl Please don't start to cry.
I'm sorry and I feel bad inside you know why.
We can work this out.
We don't have to scream or shout.
You're my world and my air.
What I said yesterday wasn't fair.
Please forgive me you know I still love you.
Without you my world is blue.
I'll never try to yell or shout.
Next time we'll talk in a polite way and work it out.

I Love Her

I have a girl and she's special to me.
Her love is unique and truthfully.
Sometimes I say things yet she finishes my line.
She reads me like a book and that's fine.
There are no secrets between us any more.
The love I feel for her I've never felt it before.
She's my heaven and earth cause she has my heart.
Her words to me Is like poetry and fine art.
My girl is the one I have always prayed for.
She's the girl in my dreams that I adore.
Her smile lights up the sky in the middle of the night.
I feel like I'm on cloud nine when she holds me tight.
My baby is very beautiful and kind to me.
In my heart I love her for eternity.
Her eyes are like stars in the sky.
I love her and I never will deny.
She's all I ever could want or need.
Without her! My heart would begin to bleed.

Playful Days

My son likes to play with me some days.
My wife said it's funny to see you in such playful ways.
We play with our fantasies; there's still a child part inside of me.
The whole house becomes everything what we wanted it to be.
Today we pretended to be peter pan and captain hook.
We're playing like it's a story out of a book.
Yesterday he was an Indian chief.
I was a trespasser and a thief.
We use swords to fight as a royal knight.
Against dragons and beast we'll fight with all our might.
Tomorrow we're superheroes that save the day with our powers.
We play at night or even in the morning hours.
Some time we fly kites or even color together.
The imported thing is I love my family forever.
My wife enjoys watching us play.
She said, you so good with our son in every kind of way.
All day playing is not the way my son.
We need to do our work after that we have some fun.
So lets clean up the toys and put them back where they belong.
Don't worry my son there will be plenty days to play or sing a
song.

Put On The Fire

The weather is gets colder and the wind starts to blow.
The nights last longer and it's raining also.
Fall is a season of every year.
Lets put on the fire my dear.
Feel the warmth of the flames; the house is warm and nice.
With you I'm always in paradise.
Ever season of the year we're now together.
That makes our love stronger and better.
Come sit with me by the fire it's cold outside so I'll hold you tight.
Under a blanked we're drinking some champagne tonight.
Baby I love you no matter where we are.
You're unique like a falling star.
Let this night be dark and cold.
This night will be in our memories, till we're grey and old.
I never had a love so perfect like this.
I snuggle close to give you a passionate kiss.
The fire makes our bodies warm with desire.
I'll bring you to cloud nine or even higher.
Let's make love my dear; I want you bad.
You're the best thing in my life I ever had.

I'll Never Leave

Let me make you feel all right.
In the early morning and all through out the night.
I give my love to you every day.
Without a word I have to say.
I'll make sure that you'll never get hurt any more.
Without you my heart would be broken and sore.
Sweetheart I live my life completely and only for you.
There's no better love then yours that feels so true.
Your love is like a rainbow after it rains.
I feel your heart while your blood is pumping through my veins.
This love is like a magic charm.
For you I would lose a leg or even an arm.
You're so good and understanding for me.
That's why my love is unconditionally.
I knew it from the first moment I seen your eyes.
Now we're together in a newfound paradise.
I'll never let you go or even let you leave my side.
God is here for our guide.
Baby I know you feel the same way too.
There will never be another for me, just only you.

An Unforgivable Mistake

I don't want to lose you.
Without you I don't know what to do.
My heart will have so much pain.
It would drive me insane.
My heart would break in two.
My love is very deep for you.
I knew I made an unforgivable mistake.
Don't let this be the end for God sake.
To hurt you! That wasn't my goal.
Girl you have my heart and soul.
I messed up! And it feels bad inside of me.
I do love you and I'll prove it you'll see.
You're my angel that showed me the way.
Let us try once more time okay.
I don't want to end our love.
It was me I didn't trust you so I gave you a shove.
I need a little more time, I didn't want to go real fast.
Let us try again so our love will forever last.
My love is still here it never went away.
Baby I still love you forever and a day.

Last Time

This is the last time I'll give my love.
I also told this to the Lord above.
This one girl has my heart and soul.
With out her my world is not whole.
If we should ever through any reason fall apart.
I would never lose her love out of my heart.
For her I would leave everything I have here behind.
I have already made up my mind.
Without her there's no meaning in my life.
When I'm in heaven I'll wait for her till she arrives.
My love for her is very deep.
There're nights that I can't sleep.
I'll wait an eternal lifetime to be by her side every night.
She feels the same way to so I know everything will be all right.
My heart will never let her go.
I love her and I want to let her know.
It was like heaven when I found her for the second time.
I don't want to sound possessive but I hope she will be mine.
Baby you're all I want and you complete me with all my needs.
Without your love my heart only bleeds.

Is Friendship Like Gold?

A lie is never honest or polite.
It's because your mind and words don't collide right.
The truth will come out anyway.
I can hear you lying in the words you say.
Don't you know by now that you're hurting me?
Seems you don't care properly.
Walking away from you problems isn't the best thing.
When you needed help why didn't you just give me a ring.
A phone call brings you close by.
You didn't I wonder why?
Well is this the end?
Is it true you aren't any more my friend?
That's too bad for you.
I take friendship for gold something what you didn't do.
When you want to say goodbye.
Keep in mind I'm not the one that will cry.
The blame is not on me.
I could be a friend for eternity.
You want to keep lying on the same track.
Then I'll say I won't take you as a friend back.
It's your choice if you want to change that lying part.
Maybe then I can forgive you and take you back into my heart.

Never Been Happier

I give to you my love complete.
That's the reason why I can't drink nor eat.
When you're not with me at night.
I would cry because I want to hold you tight.
You're everything for me.
A kiss or a touch is like electricity.
People say I've changed in a lot of ways.
I wouldn't leave my house for days.
I'm in no mood to go out with a friend.
It seems that my mood slowly fade away to a certain end.
Girl I don't care you are the one for me.
My love for you is unconditionally.
I've never been happier before.
Your love is like the seas that roar.
You and your son are like angels in heaven above.
I know you both give me a special love.
I'm glad that things worked out so well.
We can talk about everything without having to scream or yell.
Baby I'll never let you go out of my life.
I'm proud that you wanted to be my wife.

Forever Monster Free

I'm hiding under the blankest after every sound.
Sweating and I'm scared my heart starts to pound.
There're monsters in my room I heard them before.
It's true they came out of my closet door.
I've seen the boogieman in there.
He was crawling around everywhere.
His eyes light up in weird colors at night.
I don't want to look I hold my pillow tight.
Late at night I was yelling for my daddy with a very loud shout.
I was so afraid I screamed my lungs out.
My daddy runs to my room and he sets with me.
He said; I could make your room monster free.
I'm not only your daddy but also a superhero you'll see just wait.
I'll protect you I'm not afraid it will be great.
I seen my daddy he took a sword and walked around.
He said to me (shush) please make no sound.
He opened the closet door and started to fight.
From that moment the monsters left in a terrible fright.
He said to me; my son your room is forever monster free.
When you think they'll come back again just call for me.
I went to sleep and I never heard them no more.
I know it's because of my daddy he's my superhero that I adore.

My Love For You

You know I love you so.
You mean more to me then you'll ever know.
I hear you I feel you and I miss you.
And you know I do.
With all my heart there's no need to question.
We share our love with a special connection.
I found love for you that I want to share.
Because this love I have for you is very rare.
There's something you don't understand.
I want to be your man so I ask today for your hand.
I Love you with all of my heart.
I never want us to be torn apart.
I want to build a home with you.
And bring us love and joy forever through.
This is how much I have love for you, every time.
My whole heart I give to you, because you're mine.

Two Sweetest Things In My Life

I never guessed.
I would be so blessed.
The Lord gave me a son.
I never thought of having one.
God also gave me you.
Now I'm stuck to you like glue.
My life is so complete and fulfilled right now.
I really don't know how.
I know I love my two sweetest things with all my heart.
I'll never let us be torn apart.
You two were sent to me from the Father in the sky.
I can't tell a lie or I'll die.
You complete me more ways than any one.
I even love your son.
So please baby believe me when I say.
(TIAMO) "I love you" forever and a day.

Songs In My Head

When I'm at home.
I feel totally alone.
I turn the cd's on to hear our songs that set me free.
Right here by my side is where you need to be.
I can feel our love through the songs that I play.
And the sun is shining through my window with a bright ray.
It warms up my heart and soul.
It's because of you my sweetheart; you make me whole.
Everyone gives a good opinion so clear.
Hold on to that angel and you'll never have fear.
You and I are ment to be.
All the people say obviously.
Without you I would be lost.
I'll love you no matter what it cost.
I'll play our songs till you arrive.
I love you forever you are my love of my life.

Good Morning

I woke up to the break of dawn.
I turned over; and I was glad you weren't gone.
I was so happy to see your smile.
Then I lay close; and we held each other for a while.
Then I stood up and made coffee for two.
I told her, Baby I love you.
We both knew that I had to go.
But before I left I let her know.
Baby I'll see you tonight I'll promise you this.
Then I leaned over and gave her a little kiss.

Daydream Believer

My mind is drifting off to outer space.
All I see is the smile on your face.
For a lot of people it's hard to understand.
I can feel the touch of your hand.
Thoughts of yesterday are running through my head.
I still remember everything we discussed and we said.
The way you make me feel right from the start.
Shows me enough! Cause you gave me love straight from your heart.
I'll never send your feelings of love away.
Let me pray that we love each other forever and a day.
Call me a daydream believer cause I am.
I love you so much I just want to be your man.

Sweet Child Of Mine

I love you my son forever and a day.
All day long I love to see you play.
I love to hear you and see you smile.
Even just for a little while.
I have a picture of you carried in my heart.
I'll close my eyes to see you; when the world tries to tear me apart.
That picture is in my soul for me to hold.
I wrap it around me close when the nights get cold.
I'll treat you better than your real daddy would do.
Please be happy and never sad, cause I love you.
When you've done something wrong.
Your mom or I will stand here very strong.
I know you'll listen that time of the day.
When I have something to say.
When I have no choice.
I'll raise my voice.
I hope you understand when you can.
Cause I do it all for the love, my little man.

A Walk With You

We went for a walk along the seashore.
Cause you're my baby that I adore.
Walking in the sand hand and hand together.
God I'm so glad that I'm your man forever.
Sitting on a blanket on the sandy ground.
Listening to the waves cause we love that sound.
We look at all the stars way up in the sky.
They're far away looking down on you and I.
The moon is very pretty and bright.
It's such a beautiful and delightful sight.
I never want this moment to leave.
If it did I couldn't breathe.
I'm lost when you're not by my side.
When I don't have you, I have little or no pride.
So to you my love I have to say.
I'm here to stay; my love will never fade away.

Never Doubt My Love

You always say everyday to me.
I love you for eternity.
But if you want to go you may.
But the truth is baby I don't want you to run away.
Still you don't understand after all these years.
That I'll never run! I'll stand strong against our fears.
Doesn't matter what you look like your beautiful to me.
It's my heart you gain unconditionally.
Don't give my love back not tomorrow or today.
Seems you don't get it I love you in every way.
Never doubt my love that I have for you baby.
I'll never leave you; I've said it many times lately.
I'll never run from the love I have within.
I feel you love right through my skin.
You know it's the inside I care for.
Baby I love you what do you want more?
I gave everything I had; now and always.
So don't look sad but put a smile back on that face.
I Love you forever and beyond time.
My love for you is inscribed in my heart like a rhyme.

Forever In My Heart

You're the love of my life and my search to destiny.
I'll search from now till the end of eternity.
You're the one that I'll love forever.
We both know we'll be soon together.
No distance can tear us apart.
You'll stay forever in my heart.
You're the one I have been longing to hold for years.
When I hold you I can feel we both want to burst into tears.
I know now I made the right decision for me.
The past is gone; a bright future is all I see.
I'm in love and I will not let my heart stray way.
Our love is unconditional, forever and a day.
Come in my arms and let me embrace you tight.
Let me hold you through out this beautiful night.
I know I'll love you all my life.
Don't be afraid when I ask you, baby will you be my wife?

Kiss Your Past Goodbye

Goodbye to my past I think it's the best.
I finally can let it all rest.
All the things I felt before.
Aren't here any more.
All the troubles I had in my life.
I cut them out with a knife.
I don't even want them back.
I'm going to stay on the right track.
Life feels so great now.
And it's never to late to take a vow.
I'll kiss my past goodbye tonight; everything is going to be all right.
Soon I'll be with my baby, when I take an airplane flight.
Tomorrow I have you by my side forever.
I can't wait till we're back together.
My past is now all history.
Cause no one can break our love, its unconditionally.

Bus Ride

Standing at the bus stop, and the sun is hot like fire.
You're already burning and filled with desire.
We stepped up to get on the bus and walked to the rear.
Then you started to kiss and touch my neck without any fear.
Through my pants she was stroking my privet part.
I could feel the rhythm of my beating heart.
My zipper went down and she stroked my thighs.
I could see the love in her eyes.
Make love with me! And don't you stop.
The only position we could do was she on top.
The bus driver is so devious.
Cause he was looking at us.
Slowly I pushed her up and down and deep within.
She wants to moan but she couldn't so she digs her nails in my skin.
It turns us on that people are looking our direction.
It makes our blood boil with satisfaction.
Sweat is on our bodies from making love.
I said; I love you baby, I can't say it enough.
When we both surrender by a climax.
Our love is better than any nasty kind of sex.
Then she lay on my chest.
Just for a little while to rest.
Baby I love you every time I'm inside.
But here's the end of our bus ride.

Beyond Beautiful

You're so beautiful to me.
Baby I love you cant you see.
I won't run away.
Not tomorrow or today.
I only care for the inside of your soul and heart.
I loved you right from the start.
You took my heart and soul away.
And you gave your heart to me that day.
Also your son is a part of my life.
Baby; May I ask you to be my wife.
So why don't we marry and be a family.
I'll make you happy that why God choose me.
God said; now you have an angel of your own.
And this angel won't let you be alone.

After Dinner

I received a phone call from my baby last night.
She asked me for dinner and I said all right.
She brought me to this lovely place.
There she kissed me and touched my face.
Come sit next to me and let me hold you tight.
We'll sit by the window so we can see the moonlight.
I poured some champagne that was chilled on ice.
Oh my God it tasted so nice.
We left after dinner and went for a walk.
We went to the park so we could talk.
I looked in her eyes as she looked in mine.
I said; oh babe you look so fine.
The stars were shinning so bright in the warm summer night.
We found a nice spot and gazed at the stares while I held her tight.
Our love is like the stars in the sky.
We both love each other and that's no lie.
The stars are such a beautiful sight.
We watched the sunrise till the early morning light.
We made love while we saw a falling star.
You're the love of my life, forever yes you are.

A Weekend For You And I

We went for a ride by the countryside at morning light.
We wanted to spend a weekend for two we found a cabin that
night.
The cabin looks great and it's surrounded with beautiful trees.
On the other side it has a nice ocean to see.
We set on the steps, to watch the moon as it set.
I could of cried cause every thing was so perfect.
We made a nice fire while were laid down side by side that night.
We're sipping on our wine and we agreed every thing is all right.
I turned to her and she gave me a grin.
She said; come here baby and lets make love that's no sin.
We love each other so deep and true.
I want you to marry me and lets become one not two.
Then I saw heaven in her eyes.
That brought me to a newfound paradise.
Strange but it seems.
I saw her already in my dreams.
I know what I want in life that's why I'm not in doubt.
Let me tell it to the world while I shout.
Baby I love you with all I have forever and a day.
I'm here to stay and never walk away.
People hear me holler in the middle of the night.
I love my baby I know I'm right.
I look and held her in my arms so close and we both started to cry.
I need her in my life; without her I would die.
So come and sit by the fire and hold me tight.
I'll never let you go, your staying in my sight
I'll stand forever by your side.
Like the moon that draws the tide.

Can't Stop Thinking About You

When we're making love it feels like were in heaven above.
I want a lifetime to show you unconditional love.
One night won't be enough for you and I.
We're flying so high; Feels like we're going through the sky.
I can't get my head around you any more.
Can't bear living without you the one I adore.
I won't stop thinking about you.
You're my life if you only knew.
Seems that time is standing still today.
I know where there's a will there's a way.
Seems like every day you amaze me with something new.
You take my breath away and you know this is true.
It will be more then you and I together.
We also have a son that we'll love forever.
I'll love you till the day I pass away.
My love is so strong that I have to stay.

Our Love Is Far Beyond This Place

We have Fantasies of being in the shower or at the sea.
For more than an hour or three.
Thinking of making love in a room or on the floor.
Or even against the wall or a door.
Kissing your neck stroking your hair.
God I wish I could be there.
We're so far apart.
But I feel your heartbeat in my heart.
We're making love in our minds like you're here with me.
Strange like it seems, yet it feels like its reality.
I feel your body close to mine.
It's Gods work it's a sign.
Our love is far beyond this place.
Come here baby let me embrace you by your waist.
I want to make real love with my soul mate.
It would be awesome and very great.
Then I can hold her very tight.
Until its the end of every heavenly night.

Because Our Love Is So Much

Forever in love you and I.
And we both know why.
Our hearts beat together so fast.
We both know it will stand forever and last.
I'll even walk through an autumn rain.
It's my heart that you will gain.
I'll stand in the winters freezing snow.
Love is the reason that I can't let you go.
When we're together our body's touch.
We know we stay together forever, because our love is so much.
Don't give up hope on distant love or roads that seem so long.
Hold on to hope to make the weakness strong.
Your far away my desert rose, too far to kiss goodnight.
I miss her smile in the morning sunshine and her afternoon
delight.
I need her smile, her touch, and her love to fill up all my days.
Help me to live, to see, to feel, I need her tender ways.
Dreams of love then bring them home.
Hold on tight to your dreams of hope and never let them roam.

You're so Good To Me

As I walk in the meadow I see you standing there.
Off in the distance my heart pounds with a feeling I want to share.
My mind wonders in anticipation of you touch.
Your kiss last forever I love you so much.
You always know what to do and what to say.
God I love you, you're so good to me in every way.
I'll never set you free and I'll never put you through misery.
You're in my heart for now and eternality.
You know this is true.
So we'll never be blue.
You give me so much love even when I'm sad.
That's why I have no room for anything else then you in my head.

Never Forget My Love

I'll love you every day.
More then words can say.
I'll Love you more then there's stars in the sky.
No matter when they're near or far for you I would die.
You make me smile.
For you I'll cross every mile.
From the moment I met you.
I'll love you forever true.
Never forget my love not even a day.
I know you won't! Cause for that I'll pray.
God heard your prayers right to the end.
I'm going to be your guardian angel that God will send.
Strange like it seems!
You've seen me everyday in you dreams.
I can't stop! My love is so strong.
I know where our hearts belong.
Together forever you'll be with me.
Cause God has granted our prayers for eternity.

What's A Friend?

A friend is to be there when you're in need.
To be there when your heart starts to bleed.
To comfort you when you're feeling ill.
Not to just sit and be still.
When you ask for help and your friends come.
That's a real friend and not some bum.
A friend is there no matter where you are.
They really are never that far.
So just pick up the phone.
Your friends will never let you be alone.
When you tell your friends to go away.
Just remember you're the one who pushed them astray.
So hold on to your friends as long as you can.
Cause Friendships can slip right through your hand.

Being A Friend Is Hard

I have this temper that gets in my way.
Sometimes it scares my friends away.
People just push and shove me to no end.
All I want to be is their friend.
I tried to help a friend today.
All they could say was go a head and be that way.
So this friendship is fading apart.
I really don't want that I love them in my heart.
I can't help them when they don't listen to me.
So I'll just sit back and wait and see.
I hope they don't get hurt in the end.
I'll be here cause I'm theirs friend.

Friends Never Last

Real friends are there for you when you're sad and blue.
Now I'm sad but where are you?
Real friends never treat you bad.
They are there for you when you're sad.
Still I sit here all alone.
My heart tells me you're like stone.
Are you that friend that never last?
I can forget you like the rest in my past.
Why need friends if they leave and go.
It only breaks my heart real slow.
Do you really want to hurt me?
Or do you want me to cry for eternity?
I wonder are all you promises a lie?
And if they are then answer me why.
Friendship with lies will never last.
Now you belong like the rest in my past.

Its Saturday I Can't Wait

I'm glad the week is over and that Friday has come to an end.
Going to get out yes were going to party so I call all my friends.
It's Saturday in the city and it feels so right.
Finally we're going out we have a party all night.
I worked all week hard for so long.
Now Saturday is coming let the groove come on.
I like to party till the sun comes up in the mornings glow.
Dancing and drinking with my darling real slow.
It's the end of the week and I'm craving for this music beat.
It's Saturday night and I'm dancing in the street.
I need to get down to the weekend sound.
And baby! Shake that booty to the ground.
Can't stay home I need to hear some music with my baby in my
sight.
Get ready cause here I come for a Saturday party all night.

My Baby Shows Me So Much Love

When I'm down and feeling blue tonight.
My baby said come here you it will be all right.
She said think of me and I'll be there.
You know this is for sure you can feel me touching you hair.
You can feel me in your heart.
Even when were apart.
You can hear me speak to you in your mind.
Cause you can feel me as I do you all the time.
So every thing will be all right.
Cause you and I never fight.
Nothing can come between us were too strong for that.
Come here baby and lets have a good chat.
That should give you a sign.
Our love is not blind.

Candice Loves Her Man

I have this feeling that lies deep in my head.
People want me away from my girl not love but hate her instead.
They say wake up from that fantasy of love.
Come back to us and bring your head above.
I said to my friends; I love my girl with all my heart.
My friends won't leave me alone they didn't like my girl from the start.
If they don't understand that I love my girl with my whole soul.
Then they can all back up cause I'm not under there control.
I'm not leavening her; our love is real strong.
They can't be my friends because they all want to do me wrong.
I will not sit down and listen to them cuss.
So my friends this is the end for us.

I Tried To Call

I picked up the phone.
While Dialing your number I prayed you're at home.
But all I hear is a tone in my ear.
Please pick up I feel so alone right here.
This is not right.
I didn't speak to you cause I worked all night.
Can't stop thinking of you.
That's so hard to do.
Now I'm lying in my bed alone.
The T.V is on but the color is gone.
I'll try to call you again tonight.
Cause I need to know that you're all right.
Then you picked up the phone.
I hear your voice with a lovely tone.
My hard beats fast cause you're online.
Baby I've been waiting for a long time.

After All Those Years

I'm telling you this is kismet.
All of our memories I didn't forget.
Sometime we talked and joked all night.
From that moment I knew my heart was right.
Now we're together at last.
I found the love of my life that I met in my past.
Never knew it was that girl from my past until today.
I thought I'd never meet her because she's far away.
I knew this was right and it couldn't be wrong.
On the first day I felt my love was already strong.
I felt it in my soul; and I heard it in my heart.
Our two hearts were bonded from the start.
I believe that God had listen to your entreat.
Because he felt our hearts beat.
It's weird that we found each other after all these years.
Now we're crying together with happy tears.
I promise this time not to let you go!
After all these years I can finally say; I love you so.

From The First Moment

From the first moment I already knew.
My love would only be for you.
What you mean to me you'll never know.
What I feel inside I'll soon let it show.
God send me to you like an angel from above.
He knew I could give you such perfect love.
This is love that we share.
There's nothing that even could compare.

God Knew We Were Ment To Be

I went on a boat trip that I'll never forget.
Because that's the first time we met.
God knew we were ment to be.
He said: you'll share a life with her for eternity.
The memories are always in my head.
I still remember the things we said.
I never knew I would meet her again.
I remember that we joked and she liked it back then.
She didn't change a bit, not even a part that I remember.
She took my heart back in the middle of November.
It ended so short and that's my regret.
But I found her again on the Internet.
I won't let her go not any more.
I finally found the love that I really adore.

Leaving On A Jet Plane

All my bags are packed; I'm ready to go.
I'm standing' outside your door and I'll miss you so.
I hated to wake you up to say see you girl.
You're everything you're my perfect pearl.
The taxi's waiting he's blowing his horn.
I hate to go my heart feels like it's torn.
Already I'm so lonesome I could die.
But I wont let you see me cry.
Hold me like you never held me before.
Babe I love you so much you're the one that I adore.
I'm leaving but I'll be back soon with you.
No matter where I'm going my heart stays true.
I'm telling you; for me you're everything.
When I'm back would you wear my wedding ring?
She burst to tears and said; "yes I will" yet to bad you have to leave.
Oh baby let me kiss you one more time but very brief.
You know I'm coming back so wait for that day.
Close your eyes and I'll be on my way.
Dream about the days that may appear.
Remember in your heart I'm always near.
Baby you know I have to leave today.
I love you forever that is the last thing I'll say.

I Want To Be Your Man Forever

Baby can't you see.
That we where destine to be.
All day long there's no one in my mind, but you.
I couldn't think of anyone else this is true.
You mean everything to me; don't let my heart bleed.
Because you're all I'll ever need.
You're such a pretty woman and you make my heart sing.
I want to put on your finger, a beautiful wedding ring.
Our lives will be so special together.
Baby, take my hand I want to be your man forever.
Every time I look into your eyes I see.
The one I want beside me for eternity.
You've made me the happiest man that I ever dreamed of.
So set up a date and take my name and let me show you love.

One Last Time

It's hard to take a breath.
Cause my heartbeats me to death.
It's because I love you.
I give to you my love brand new.
Can't stop any more.
When I can't be with you my heart feels sore.
I'll never hurt you from this day.
It's not a nice thing when the feeling isn't okay.
What I feel can't be wrong.
My true feelings are so strong.
Baby let me try one last time.
That will prove you're mine.
I wont hurt you not again.
When I do I am less then a real man.
I know I hurt you from the start.
Yet today I want to give you all of my heart.
Baby will you join my hand for eternity.
Cause in my heart I believe we where ment to be.

I Know We Will Last

I Love you forever and a day.
Lets promise never to walk away.
I love you so much.
All I want is to feel your touch.
Wish you where here with me like yesterday.
I hope you can see it clear that I want you here to stay.
My heart is beating so fast.
I know our love will forever last.
Let us join hands tomorrow.
I know we'll be happy without any sorrow.
The first time we met our hearts where beating so fast.
That's why we knew our love would last.
That first kiss; it was like magic that held us together.
I don't want to miss a thing; I want to remember everything forever.
Let me stand with you every night and day.
I love you so much; and I never want you to walk away.

We're Not Perfect

When I seen your eyes.
I knew I couldn't tell any lies.
You're to good to be true.
You make my life so freaking new.
And there's no regret.
Not even from the day we met.
I just want to spend a lifetime with you.
That's why I give my love to you brand new.
We go through good times and bad times.
We're connected with our body, soul and even our minds.
We're not perfect in any way.
But one thing is we both know we want to stay.
This love is for a lifetime for you the one I adore.
Because my love is stronger then it was before.
I love you baby each and every day.
We know our love is pure in every way.

The Way You Are

Baby will you please look at me.
Then tell me what you see.
I love you the way you are.
Your smile is like a bright star.
Looking into your eyes brings me to heaven all the time.
Your touch and kisses feels so fine.
Your heart is so pure like gold.
Baby I need you to hold.
What do I see? A little boy that's coming to me.
Oh my God he said! Daddy I love you for eternity.
I started crying with happy tears.
I know when we meet I'll have no fears.

It's So Clear

When we're together our words aren't always the same.
Sometimes it feels like it's a game.
I feel you so well like a real touch.
Some people don't understand and say we don't know much.
My heart tells me that you're the one.
When we're together were always having fun.
Even when we don't get along and we have a fight.
We both stay together and talk it out even when it takes all night.
We always seem to work things out.
We never will scream or shout.
So baby will you please come here.
I need you tonight it's so clear.
I love you so much baby can't you see.
Hold me and kiss me and say sweet words to me.
You're the woman I'm dreaming of.
God sent you to me from heaven above.
Never leave my side cause you're the one I adore.
You mean so much to me, No! You mean so much more.

Thanks To The Keeper

When I hold you in my arms tonight.
There's a soft bright moonlight.
When I look into your eyes.
It makes me feel like I'm in paradise.
I have all I'll ever need.
I know this because of my heartbeat.
When I hold you in my arms I start to cry.
And God is watching from the sky.
He's smiling down on us from his Heavenly thrown.
He whispers in my ear never leave her alone.
He sure knew what he was doing because he's so clever.
That's why he joined these two hearts together.
All those wars he said aren't better then your love.
That's why I bow my head to the keeper in heaven above.
So enjoy your new life that I gave you both today.
Follow this new path of life, but never stray away.

Finally I'm Free From All This Misery

I don't want to be here.
No one else can see it clear.
Now I'm free.
From all this pain and misery.
Someone is trying to tear me apart.
Yet I know I love this girl with all my heart.
I know where I want to be.
When I'm with her I feel free.
Every person deserves a good partner in there life.
Everything is going to be better cause soon she's my wife.
Love is the key.
My heart burns for her for eternity.
Every morning I'll say that I love her forever and a day.
Just to let her remember; that my love will never stray way.
There's no one else that may touch me.
Cause I love my baby so dearly.
She makes my dreams come true.
I'll say to her; my happiness is all because of you.

God Knew What He Has Done

It was no accident that I found you.
Someone had a hand in it long before we knew.
I can't believe you're back in my life once more.
Every day there is a new surprise for us to explore.
As I take a look at you tonight.
I know everything is going to be all right.
God knew what he has done.
He joined these two hearts together and made them one.
I have it all I'll ever need.
Without you my heart would bleed.
A soft moonlight is shining on your face.
It takes my breath always while I drift of to space.
Thanks to the keeper of the stars above.
I'm blessed with an angel that gives me so much love.
Do I really deserve a treasure like you?
It must be, because God let our love grow strong and new.

I'm Going To Meet You Soon

I know this is real.
This feeling that I feel.
It's because of you.
I finally found a love that's so true.
You're my sunshine after the rain.
You take away all my pain.
I lose my mind cause you're not close by.
Sometimes all I do is cry.
I'm going to meet you some day.
Nothing can take my dreams away.
I'm so nerves to meet you I'll tell you this.
I don't know should I hug you or give you a kiss.
Our feelings will show us exactly what to do.
I'm telling you baby it will be good for us two.
Come in my arms and don't let me go.
(Crying) Baby I love you so.

I'll Find You

I love to look into your beautiful eyes.
They hypnotize me and send me to paradise.
They're saying sweet words nobody dares to say.
That's why I'm not letting you run away.
Like deja vu I feel I was always near.
That's why I kept looking for you for over a year.
In my dreams it's you I'm searching for.
But I woke up when someone slammed the door.
This is just the sign and I'll find you in any case.
I'm trying to search and find you in every possible place.
When I find you, I hope you'll be willing to be mine.
I know finding you is just a matter of time.
I'll meet you I know this for real.
Something inside of me knows how I feel.
It's like you're already in my soul.
I know this because my six senses is under control.

We Never Lost The Love

So many things I want to say.
Yet I couldn't find the words that day.
I got so many things to do.
But there's always time to say; I love you.
Time is a hard moment in our life.
A breath will be taken on the day we arrive.
I loved you from the moment we met.
Girl did you think I could ever forget.
Meeting you in that bar.
It didn't chance the way we are.
We had laughter and fun that night.
You knew it was love on first sight.
God knows the feeling that we share together.
So he created a road that would last forever.
Then he let us meet again.
This time love will never end.
He knew we never lost the love.
So he sends us an angel from above.
Soon were back as we're supposed to be.
God is now smiling down on you and me.

Love Is What We Feel

Sitting here and thinking of you.
Wondering what you're doing to.
Poems from my heart I've written them down everyday.
It's easy for me the words to find and say.
Did I tell you I love you and this is no lie?
It's your eyes and smile that lights up the sky.
Don't worry I wont leave you standing there.
My love is so strong but all this waiting just isn't fair.
It's hard when you make a golden promise to some one.
You can't take it back, because its already been said and done.
When I'm alone I wonder what should I do?
I don' t know, would you do the same thing to?
I finally found you and I don't want to be alone.
I don't like the feeling of being hurt to the bone.
Love is what we feel.
I'll be your knight in shining Armour of steel.
My love is only for you.
It's pure and so true.
Come here and let me embrace your body tight.
While I whisper in your ear: I want to make love with you tonight.

I Love You This Much

You're my moon that shines so bright.
You are my star that I want to hold all night.
You're my sunshine on my face.
You're like the planets in outer space.
You have a smile that drives me wild.
I love you so much girl and also your child.
Your eyes light up my heart.
I pray we'll never be torn apart.
I want you in my life to make me complete.
Looking at you is such a treat.
You're all I ever pray or could hope for.
Stay with me baby forever and more.
I love you this much.
I know that you like it when I speak to you in Dutch.

They Will Be The Lonely One

People say it's not love that I feel.
That's so foolish and unreal.
Cause I can feel your touch.
That gives me a sign you love me so much.
I don't listen to what people say.
It's my decision any way.
If they don't understand that I love you till the end.
It shows me I never had a real friend.
They say I'm drifting out to space; and my love is not true.
But what they don't know is I really have met you.
They will be the lonely one.
When they want love it will never come.
I want to thank you for the things you've done for me.
I'm never going to doubt that you're the one for eternity.

Beginning Of A New Start

I want to call you in the middle of the night.
When I hear you all I want to do is hold you tight.
I know these feelings from my heart.
This is a beginning of a brand new start.
I know you can feel my pain.
Because this feeling we have is the same.
I'll do everything for our love.
The feeling that you gave completes me enough.
My heart races fast like a train.
And my mind is calling your name.
Baby I love you so bad that I could cry.
Then I'll fall to my knees and pray to the Lord in the sky.
I'm asking the Lord; never let my love fade away.
But instead to let it grow stronger ever day.
I'll never find love so pure like this.
Baby I can't wait for our first real kiss.

My Heart Starts To Beat Like Its Brand New

My golden dreams have come true.
Now I'm here with you.
When we're together our hearts beat so strong.
I use to think I knew what love was but I was so wrong.
I used to feel like I was alone.
Soon we'll be together in our own home.
I can't fight the feeling inside of me.
It's so strong like a roaring sea.
Your smile reminds me of the sun in the sky above.
Girl you give me so much love.
And when I'm kissing you.
I can feel that our love is true.
When I'm with you and I feel your touch.
It makes my body shiver and shake so much.
I couldn't wait for the day I flown back to you.
Nobody can stop me and you know this is true.
Soon I can hold you against me.
It will be perfect like it should be.

Today Was A Lonely Day.

I was completely alone today.
My baby she had to go away.
I set by the phone and waited for it to ring.
All I heard was the sweet sound of the birds when they sing.
The clock is ticking real slowly.
I'll set down to watch the TV; cause I felt so lonely.
All I could do was think about my sweetheart.
God I hate this feeling inside of me cause it tears me apart.
Could She be coming home real soon? Well maybe!
I know my girl! She'll be all right eventually.
I went outside for a little while.
I was so upset I even walked a mile.
I felt my anger building up inside of me.
I hate this feeling because sometimes I cry so heavily.
So I walked slowly back to our house.
I was so quiet just like a little mouse.
I'll sit and wait for my darling to come home.
Even though I extremely dislike being alone.
When she walked through the door and I saw her face.
I cried to my lover and held her in a long embrace.
You're finally home! I said to her after a long lonely day.
I missed you so much! And that's all I could say.

Something Unique

We have such a special love.
That was a gift from God above.
We feel our touch from very far away.
It's something unique like a falling star; cause you don't see it
every day.
People don't understand what I mean so I'll never talk about this.
They say its Impossible to feel a far away distanced touch or a kiss.
I don't care what they think about our special love.
Girl you complete me cause you're my guardian angel from above.
The first time we met we held each other very tight.
It was a bit scary but yet it felt so right.
I won't let you go because my love is very deep.
I'll pray to God that these feelings are for us to keep.

Soft Kiss.

A soft kiss and a light moan.
All this cause my love has grown.
I search gently for your mouth for a soft kiss.
Cause there's no moment that I want to miss.
No matter how far we are.
I'll always wish on a perfect star.
Even though we have a distance before we'll come together.
We know our hearts will stay joined forever.
Soon we'll be together as one.
And we won't forget our little son.
We'll love each other for eternity.
Cause we're perfect as a family.

About the Author

Werner W.J.F Toelen, A poet writer from The Netherlands. He was born in 1977, in the north of Brabant. With his heart and soul he loves to write. The feeling he has is inscribes in his work. He's a wonderful person with a golden heart. Many people have already experience his delightful work. He has people amazed with laughter and tears.

After meeting the love of his life, he became this charming person. A fairytale came alive, with help of a friend on the Internet. The themes are about love losing love ones friendship and even mystery. With a smile he would say; come closer and know me better. Enjoy of the poetry that will warm your heart forever.

To EMMA

WISH you all The Best
on youR PATH of life

Werner W.J.F Toelen

CPSIA information can be obtained
at www.ICGtesting.com
Printed in the USA
BVHW030920201219
567307BV00001BA/16/P